PAINTWORK
A PORTRAIT OF
THE FALL

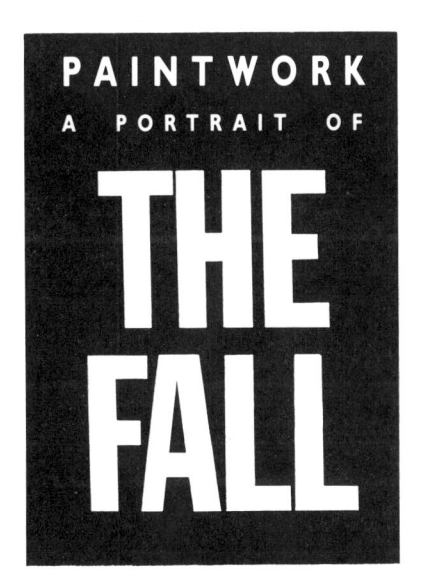

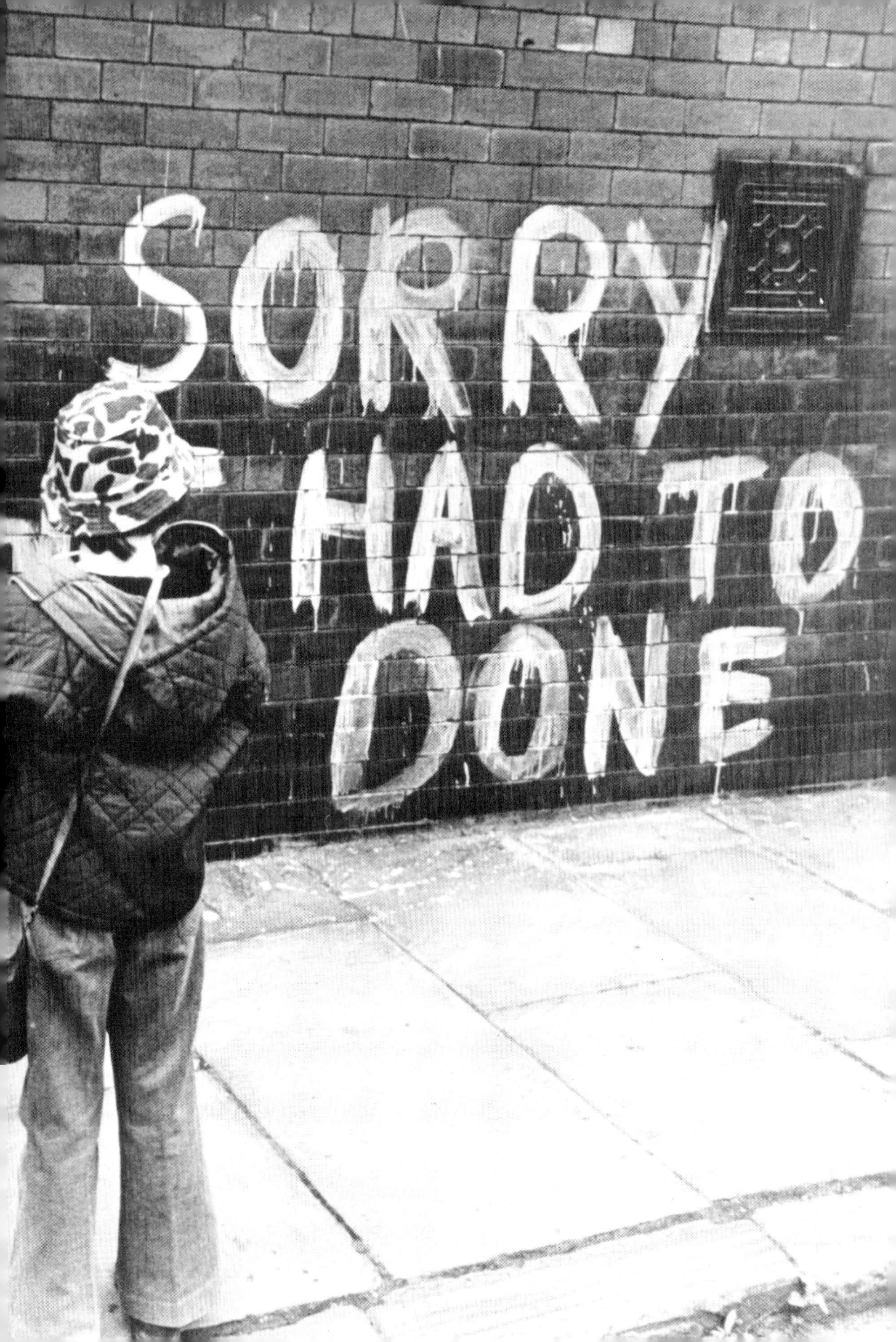
SORRY
HAD TO
DONE

PAINTWORK
A PORTRAIT OF THE FALL

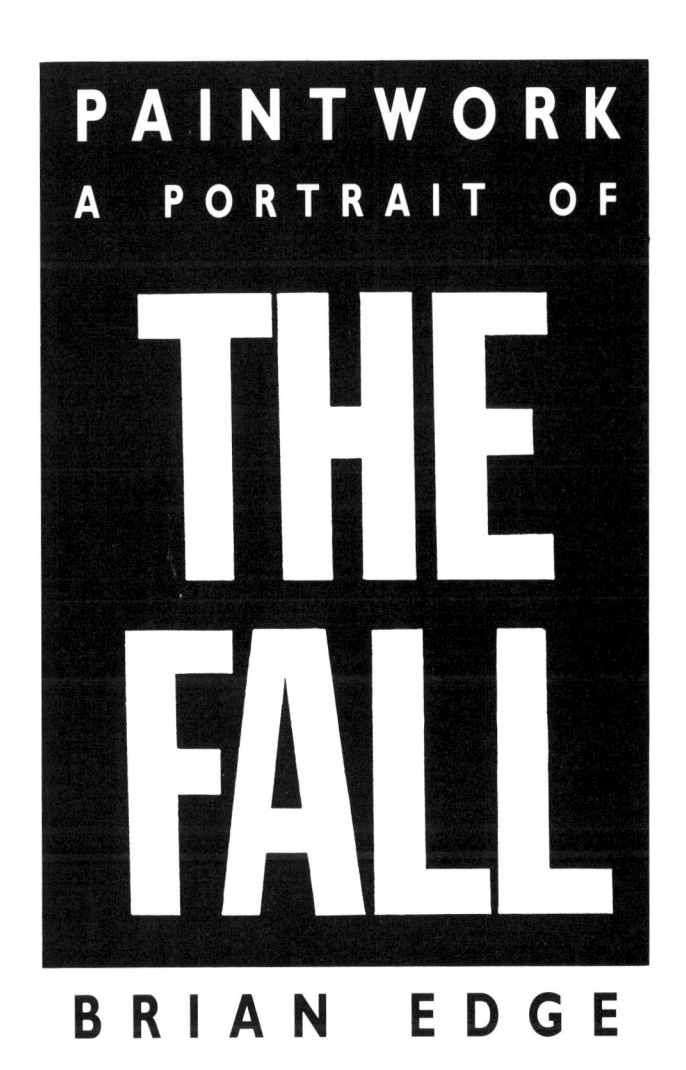

BRIAN EDGE

Omnibus Press
London/New York/Sydney/Cologne

© Copyright 1989 Omnibus Press
(A Division of Book Sales Limited)

Edited by Chris Charlesworth
Book Designed by AB3 Design
Picture Research by Debbie Dorman
Project and typesetting co-ordinated by Caroline Watson

ISBN 0.7119.1740.X
Order No: OP45210

All rights reserved. No part of this book may be reproduced in any form or by any electronic or mechanical means, including information storage or retrieval systems, without permission in writing from the publisher, except by a reviewer who may quote brief passages.

Exclusive distributors:

Book Sales Limited,
8/9 Frith Street,
London W1V 5TZ, UK.

Music Sales Corporation,
225 Park Avenue South,
New York, NY 10003, USA.

Music Sales Pty Limited,
120 Rothschild Avenue,
Rosebery, NSW 2018, Australia.

To the Music Trade only:
Music Sales Limited,
8/9 Frith Street,
London W1V 5TZ, UK.

The author would like to thank the following sources and their respective sources:

Jack Barron, Tony Clayton-Lea, Richard D. Cook, Mark Cooper, Nancy Culp, Paolo Hewitt, Barney Hoskyns, Andy Hurt, Colin Irwin, Dave Jennings, Steve Lake, Graham Lock, Gavin Martin, Barry McIlheney, Mick Middles, Tom Morton, Ian Penman, Edwin Pouncey, Sandy Robertson, William Shaw, Mat Snow, Andy Strickland, Don Watson and Frank Worrall.

Picture Credits:
Peter Anderson Back Cover, p35, 44, 46, 47(L&R), 50, 51, 52, 53, 54, 55, 68, 69, 70, 71, 72, 74, 78, 79, 80(L&R), 82, 83, 84, 85, 86, 89.
Bleddyn Butcher p38, 41, 58, 60, 61, 64, 66, 91.
Kevin Cummins p6, 8, 9, 10, 11, 12, 13, 14, 20, 21.
Jack Hickes Photos Ltd. p2.
London Features Int. Front Cover, p36, 37, 40, 48, 63(T&B), 76, 77.
Andy Phillips p88.
Barry Plummer p16, 17, 18, 19.
Paul Slattery p22, 23, 24, 25, 26, 27, 28, 29, 31, 32, 33, 34, 56, 57.

Every effort has been made to trace the copyright holders of the photographs in this book but one or two were unreachable. We would be grateful if the photographers concerned would contact us.

Typeset by Capital Setters, London.
Printed in England by Courier International Ltd., Tiptree, Essex.

CONTENTS

BACKDROP **7**

CALL YOURSELVES BLOODY PROFESSIONALS? **15**

ROCK AND POP FILTH **29**

PROLE ART THEATRE/SCHISM **39**

WORDS OF EXPECTATION **49**

GODZONE **59**

THE PAY-OFF **75**

DISCOGRAPHY **92**

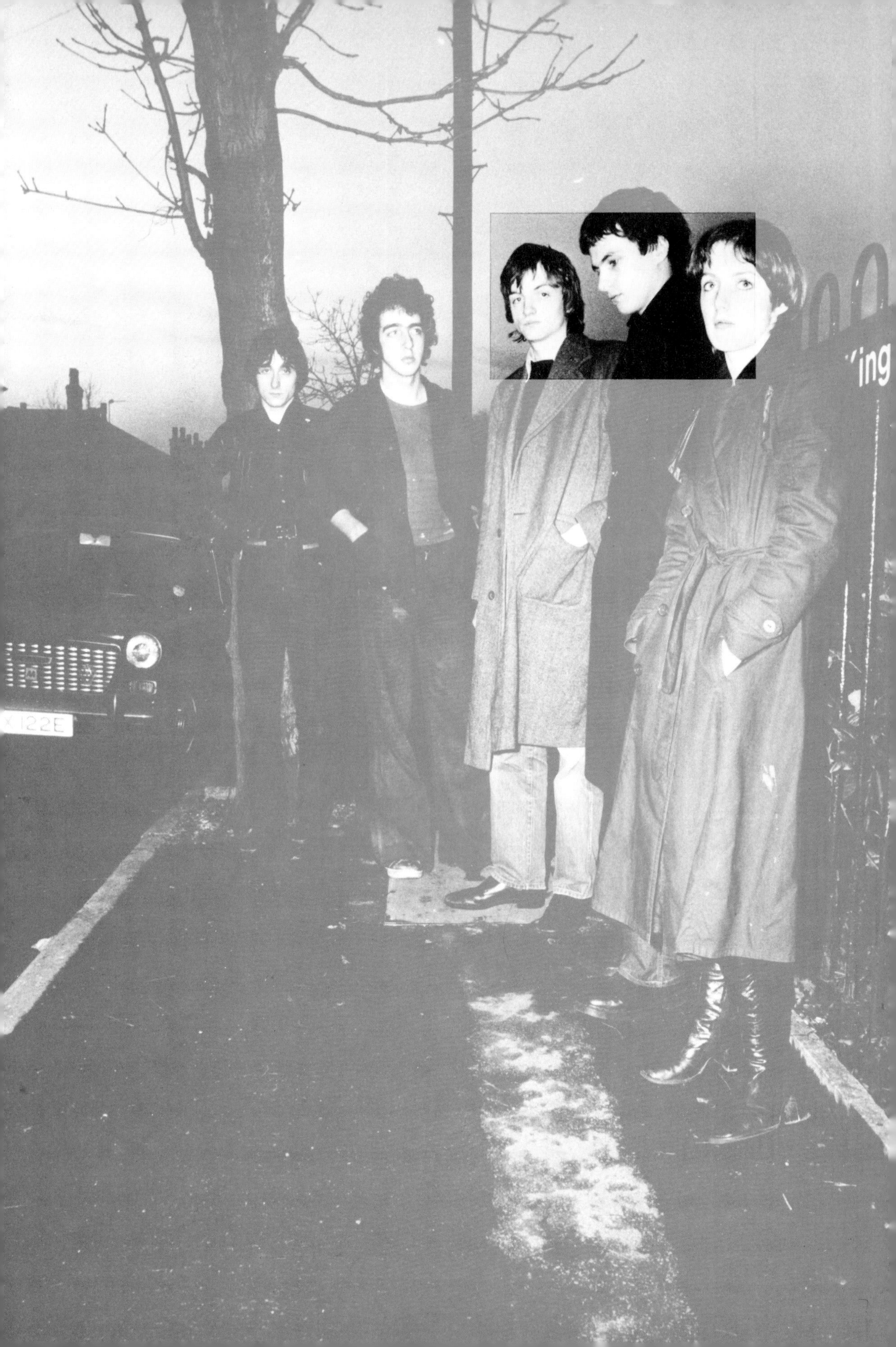

'Cut your hair or miss the boat.' – Music Scene.

CHAPTER 1
BACKDROP

By 1986, 10 years after the main event, punk had become a dirty, four-letter word. The spawn of 1976 had either recanted the faith long since or been subject to miraculous deathbed conversions, and the late-comers were denouncing their true origins faster than you could say 'God Save The Queen'. In some cases it was worse. Those still active were trying to stave off jaundices and a general air of stagnation, while the passive had been hunched over the cold, dead grate for so long they were being warmed and comforted by the hot coals of nostalgia. So much time, not enough distance.

Manchester, with its week-long 'Festival Of The Tenth Summer' in mid-July, was no different. More than just a simple nod of acknowledgement to the era's cultural importance, it was, with its candy-box assortment of musical events, exhibitions of photography and design, genre films and peripheral activities, an unabashed reminder of 'The way we were'. Or perhaps, 'How we aged graciously'.

To their credit, organisers like Factory Records boss Tony Wilson were honestly celebrating the fact that 1976 happened at all, and that it had happened for them and many others in the city of Manchester. Yet he was modest enough to concede that such a celebration could have just as easily been staged in Glasgow or Liverpool. "Or even London," he added with a smile. There's nothing special about Manchester.

The Festival's centrepiece was the G-Mex all-day music spectacular, its accent heavily on home-grown talent. New Order appeared high on the billing, so too The Smiths and The Fall. These were people who, in spite of every distraction thrust before them by the music business over the years, still chose to remain close to their roots. And where they came from and why they came as they did is now a cliché. When The Sex Pistols broke cover towards the end of 1976 there must have been a veritable traffic jam on the road to Damascus.

Mark E-for-Edward Smith, the maw and mind of the band they call The Fall, was a provincial youngster when he saw those anarchic minstrels play in his home town. So few people turned up at that first gig that Malcolm McLaren was able to greet them individually as they went in. It was the group of young punks he managed that the audience had heard tell of, for whom they had paid to see and who galvanised many among their number into action.

Opposite: Tony Friel, Karl Burns, Mark Smith, Martin Bramah, Una Baines – December 1977

Mark Smith, Una Baines, Martin Bramah, Karl Burns, Tony Friel – December 1977

At the time Mark Smith was working in Manchester Docks as a customs clerk, an office junior with a yen for The Velvet Underground, Captain Beefheart, Can, Lou Reed, Peter Hammill – anything a few miles off rock's golden highways. In Iggy Pop he had already found a hint of things to come.

"I only bought 'Raw Power' for the cover," he said, remembering the thrill of spending his first week's wages on The Stooges' first album. "When I went into Virgin Records they all sneered at me from the counter so I knew I must be on to something good."

Spurting off at a similar, energetic tangent, local sweethearts The Buzzcocks, fronted by Howard Devoto and Pete Shelley, were first to appear on an exploding Manchester scene. Like those that closely followed, they too cared not to cite such established stars as David Bowie and Marc Bolan as a source of inspiration, despite – or perhaps in spite of – their supreme influence. All abhorred the mainstream junk and tedious double-album supergroups of the early seventies.

Mark Smith, caught by the rising tide, teamed up with sympathisers Tony Friel and Martin Bramah, all of them 19 going on 20. Presently they were joined by Una Baines and Karl Burns, and together they formed The Fall. By the time The Pistols made their second and more legendary appearance at the city's Free Trade Hall early in 1977, their own band had begun to lead a typically cloistered existence. Though determined, they never ventured out of bedroom or basement, nor dared trespass on the hallowed stage. Right up to the eve of The Great Invasion Of 1977 there was still a sneaking suspicion that the noble boards really were someone else's property. As *Melody Maker*'s Barry McIlheney later discovered, it was the sight of those primitive first performances that was so instrumental in The Fall taking their music out into the open.

"I remember seeing The Buzzcocks," revealed Smith, "and thinking, 'Bloody hell! I could do better than that!' It's a cliché now, but that honestly was the attitude at the time – anyone can do it. Up until I saw The Pistols doing stuff like 'Stepping Stone' and other garage songs, the idea of us playing in public was pure fantasy."

Their début came in May, with Mark Smith as vocalist, Tony Friel on bass, Una Baines on tinny electric piano and Karl Burns on drums. The latter was recognised as being the only half-way accomplished 'musician' in the outfit, having played in a succession of cabaret and heavy metal groups since the age of 13. In the early days, while the rest of the band were acquainting themselves with their new toys and fighting against the temptation of 'doing their own thing', Karl Burns' disciplined drumming acted as the necessary anchor. Guitarist Martin Bramah, with his guillotine style of playing, admitted to modelling himself on former Television bassist Richard Hell, presently with the American group The Void-Oids. Hell later joined the ranks of punk's walking wounded, one of many old soldiers who were heard to bleat, "I invented punk rock but no one will give me credit for it!"

Increased commitment to the group led to late nights and it wasn't long before Smith, who had already refused promotion to 'manager-type', was sacked from his job for unpunctuality. Fortunately for him, the new wave was breaking. Suddenly The Fall found themselves eagerly turning out for support slots to the likes of Slaughter And The Dogs, The Worst, The Drones, and other short-lived pulp bands. Yet from the beginning The Fall viewed themselves as outsiders, often misread and disliked by their peers. Undeniably part of the blanket movement, they never regarded themselves as 'punks'.

"Punk?" said Smith with distaste. "I hate that stuff. I wouldn't have it in the house. I don't. UK Subs and stuff like that, it's beneath me. It's more pathetic than skinheads, it really is."

As they say, just because a cat is born in the coal-shed, that doesn't make it a lump of coal. Nevertheless, repeated exposure on the burgeoning 'alternative circuit' soon ensured The Fall a dedicated following they could call their own. Pursued beyond the borders of their native Lancashire, as they charmed and abused their way around the north of England, The Fall picked up additional converts including the pre-Bunnymen Ian McCulloch at Eric's, Liverpool's hive of underground activity:

Una Baines, Mark Smith – Manchester, December 1977

Martin Bramah, Mark Smith – The Ranch – Manchester, August 1977

McCulloch was so impressed by their originality that he helped hump the band's equipment around.

The Fall were a breed apart and they knew it. Yet it wasn't simply a matter of their pointed, repetitive music being streets ahead of the chainsaw guitars and unsustainable adrenalin of the mob. Neither were they singled out because Mark Smith was more a caustic raconteur than your typical affable vocalist. Like the rest of the band, his delivery was plain and unanimated, save for the odd scream or facial contortion.

Ironically, what really set them apart was their untreated appearance. Dressed on-stage and off in such ordinary articles of clothing as pullovers and corduroy trousers, The Fall suffered acutely from a credibility gap. They appeared woefully ignorant of the new vogue for black leather, bristles, studs and acne. ("Same old blank generation," moaned Smith in 'Repetition'). Unhinged by the sight of frontman Smith's lank, greasy hair, some hard-line fanzines intimated that the group didn't really belong. Ears were what they wanted, and a regulation close-cropped barnet. Smith was unamused. "Here were these kids," he fumed, "who'd been heavy metal fans six months before and they were now attacking me for having long hair."

The Fall – The Ranch, Manchester, August 1977

This wearing of collar-length hair was tantamount to being a (much-vilified) hippy, a *faux-pas* of monumental proportions. Certain commentators, however, viewed this aspect of The Fall's single-mindedness in a favourable light.

"They are shabby," wrote *NME*'s Ian Penman, "ordinary, have no 'image', but unlike certain other image-less people do not osmose any kind of urban commando *tout-suite* street chic . . . in other words they do not exploit their background."

There was nothing to lend force to the music save the words, nothing to support the words bar the music. No act, no compromise, no gimmick. Those more used to the uniforms and po-faces of London punk – The Clash, The Damned, Generation X, The Jam if you will – got a hefty shock when they first glimpsed The Fall on the cover of their second single 'It's The New Thing'. Grinning, and with fists mockingly raised in salute, the band exuded the slovenly air of a gang of cheery bricklayers, a look at odds with their radical sound. As such The Fall were a challenge, a book without a cover.

"I've figured out why I don't dress weird," Smith revealed to *NME*'s Mat Snow. "I don't dress weird because people don't talk to you when you dress weird. And I have this strong suspicion that only people who are very, very straight dress weird."

'It's The New Thing' was aimed at opportunists who, having picked up on the spurious notion that 'anything goes', abused both the spirit and momentum of the age by jumping on the punk roller-coaster. Meanwhile, Mark Smith seemed happy enough to deliver the sarcastic aside, "I wonder what is next year's thing?" Punk was barely a year old, the energy at its height, and everyone was in transports of delight at its laxative effect on the conservative music industry. Few were so disparaging as to berate the merry-makers. Yet The Fall weren't alone in their criticism of the fledgling iconoclasts and their attendant horde. The Adverts, in their song 'Safety In Numbers', exposed the new wave as being the new conformity, the latest in herding instincts, though some found this attitude overly cynical.

To the Fall it was all part of the music scene, corrupt in its omnipotence, immoral in its influence, and whose lowest levels they now inhabited. From the outset it was one of the band's major obsessions. They held it up repeatedly to ridicule, deriding it in a dozen songs, 'Music Scene' being their first broadside. A particularly memorable version of this tirade appeared on a live tape from a 1978 gig at Oldham's Tower Club. Smith and Bramah introduced the encore with glee: "This is our party piece, 10 minutes of it at least!"

Martin Bramah, Karl Burns, Mark Smith, Una Baines, Tony Friel – August 1977

Martin Bramah, Mark Smith – The Ranch, Manchester, August 1977

Half-way through, Smith paused to deliver one of his 'read-outs': "At all the gigs, you don't get in for free. When you go to the record shop you don't get it for free. In fact, you get about five pound; you put five pound on the counter: you get about half an hour. Ha-ha! Half an hour for five pound! Seven-inch, 80 pence. Eighty pence for about five minutes. But the sleeves are very nice, yes, the sleeves are very nice . . .

"Don't put your daughter on here," he concluded, motioning at the stage.

Behind the ill humour, Smith was clear in his mind why The Fall were involved in this musical uprising. "You can use primitive methods to communicate," he told *NME*'s Graham Lock. "Which is why I'm in it, because I haven't got any skills and you need a backer in most of the arts. But rock and roll is the only form where you can do that. Which is why it's beautiful. Rock and roll isn't even music really: it's a mistreating of instruments to get feelings over. And the way people abuse that dream in the music business is terrible."

It was important too for them to make an enlightened contribution, not merely take advantage of the situation. As Martin Bramah commented, "A lot of groups have got into rebelling on that silly piss artist level."

For The Fall, who had opted to remain on the scene's fringes for the duration, there would be no compromise. Ever. They were not going to poison the well. Over the decade that followed, there were few bands who would remain true to this once commonplace ideal.

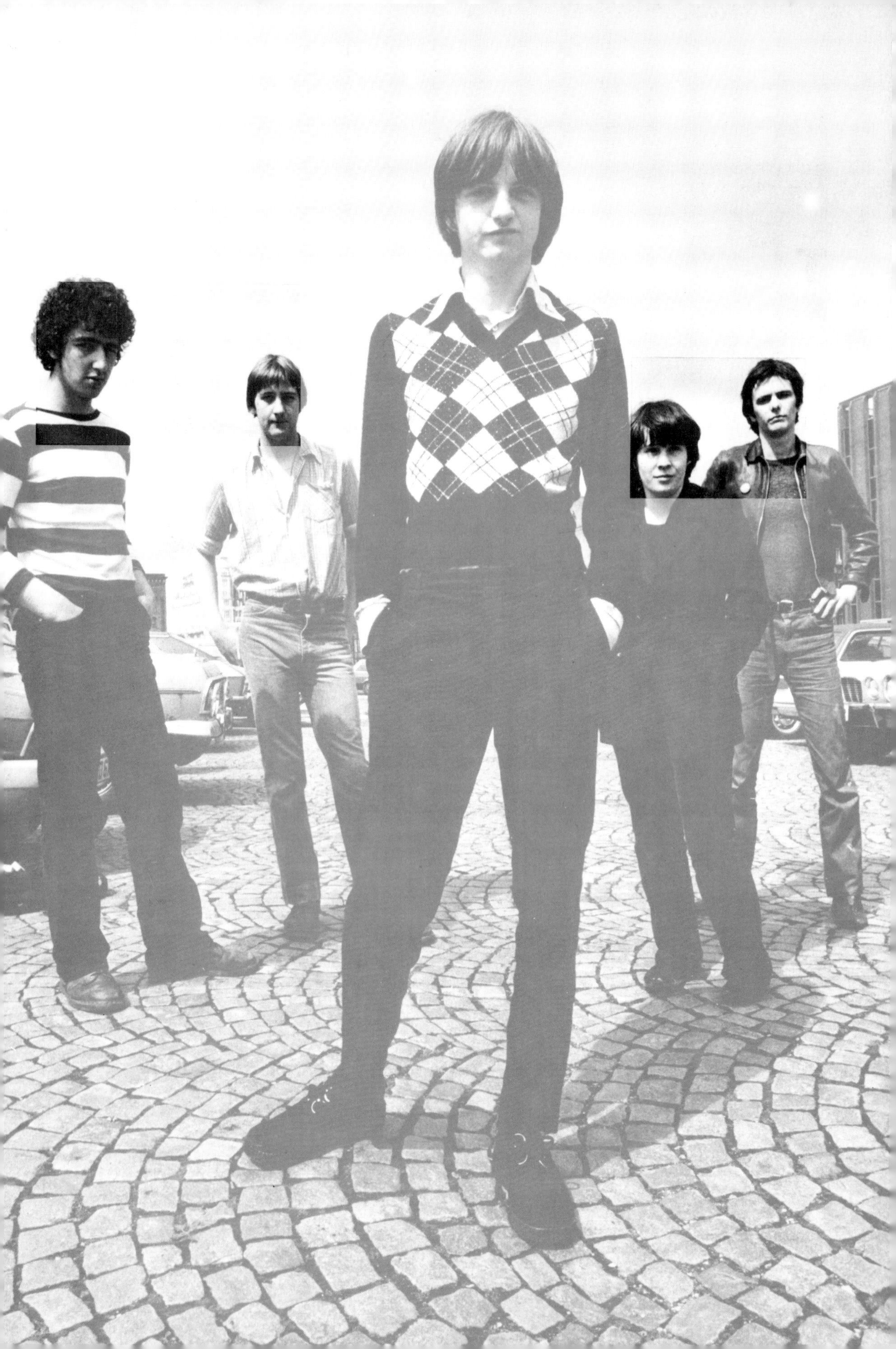

'They say with the masses, don't take any chances.' –
'Dice Man'.

CHAPTER 2
CALL YOURSELVES BLOODY PROFESSIONALS?

The Fall first appeared on record in June 1978 with the release of 'Short Circuit – Live At The Electric Circus', a limited edition blue vinyl 10-inch LP. It commemorated the demise of Manchester's Electric Circus which, on precious past Sundays had been the playground of the city's disaffected youth. Recorded the previous November by Virgin Records' mobile studio, the album captured a number of local heroes during the club's final blow-out, lasting all weekend. Buzzcocks were far and away the biggest attraction, with The Fall vying for second place alongside punk's foremost poet John Cooper Clarke, a neighbour of Smith's in Salford. Bringing up the rear, as ever, were The Drones, on this occasion out-droned by Warsaw, the band who later changed their name and their music to become Joy Division.

'Short Circuit' was an important snapshot of The Fall, capturing their first manifestation at a time when they had yet to make an impact outside their home territory. "Music of structure and insight," read Paul Morley's sleeve notes; the *NME* writer described the band as, "Science Fiction . . . Tantalising. Accusing. Compelling."

For many, the rough and grumble of 'Stepping Out' and 'Last Orders' was their introduction to the group. Radio One's John Peel, champion of the new wave, was so enthusiastic he played the tracks repeatedly on his show. Before long the band were invited to record a session for broadcasting. Over the coming years The Mighty Fall, as Peel called them, would become a regular feature.

However, two members of the original line-up were soon to depart: Tony Friel, who later formed The Passage with Dick Witts, and Una Baines. One of their final duties with the band was the recording of The Fall's début EP at Manchester's Indigo Studios that same November. Smith explained their motive.

"It was just bloody-mindedness. It just became a matter of principle to get this EP out."

Its title track, 'Bingo Master's Breakout', glimpsed at Smith's penchant for off-beat scenarios featuring our hapless citizenry. He had written it on an outing with his parents. The accompanying 'Psycho Mafia' railed against pharmaceutical companies, whom they accused of screwing up people's minds and lives with tranquillisers, all in the irreproachable name of Medicine. This, too, was one of The Fall's early passions. They could not reconcile the fact that multinational companies made millions peddling

Opposite: The Fall, August 1978

Housewives' Ruin across the globe, while an out of work pipe-fitter would get banged up in Wakefield jail for six months because traces of some heinous substance were found on his person. The band's third single, 'Rowche Rumble', in which discredited valium giants Hoffman La Roche were damned as 'Swiss gnomes dealing out potions', presented the plaintiff's case more coherently.

Their début ended with another live favourite, five minutes-plus of 'Repetition', a protracted declaration of intent – 'We've got repetition in the music and we're never going to lose it!' By comparison to the two other tracks, 'Repetition' overstayed its welcome. Not that Mark Smith ever shied away from airing his more abstruse lyrics, nor indeed had The Fall ever held back from playing such endless, rolling compositions. In fact, when the group became skilled in handling a song in this manner, they gave their most powerful performances.

'Bingo Master's Breakout' eventually saw release in August 1978, serving both to underline The Fall's presence on the independent scene and justify the increased amount of attention the new line-up was now drawing. Friel's successor, 16-year-old Marc Riley performed ably on bass, and Nico-fixated ex-art school student Yvonne Pawlett maintained The Fall's trademark of amateurish keyboard playing. Even without Baines' lyrical contributions, new songs continued to appear at a disarming rate.

As *NME*'s Ian Penman remarked at the time, "There has been a lot of interest shown in The Fall these past few weeks. Like they're low on charisma, direction, ability and everything – y'know, a lot of good points."

Penman's mockery was perhaps excusable on the grounds that The Fall were simply another band who were bringing out their first single, one of many in "the '77 shit-pile", as Smith fondly referred to it in 'In My Area'.

"Just more anti-heroes thrashing through the night," concluded Penman dismissively. "I wish that they were even nasty, or ideologically repulsive, but they're not. They are not 'humourless'. They are not 'political'. Three of them can make quite a tidy thrashing noise. One can write words which oppose but never propose. Martin would be on the dole . . . ."

Following The Buzzcocks' influential example of releasing 'Spiral Scratch' on their own New Hormones label, do-it-yourself productions were suddenly all the rage. Propagandists Scritti Politti even went so far as to quote production costs on the cover of their first release, 'Skank Bloc Bologna', to show that it was possible to put out a record without getting caught in the dangerous machinery of the music industry, and at a relatively low cost to boot. Independent labels sprang up all over the country and by the end of the seventies such labels as Stiff, Factory, Rough

Martin Bramah & Mark Smith

Trade, Fast, Small Wonder and Step Forward were all familiar names.

A penniless Fall, scoffing that other groups could only make records because they had middle-class parental patronage, approached London-based Step Forward Records, whose stock-in-trade included no-hopers The Cortinas, Chelsea, The Models and, briefly, Sham 69. As Mark Smith subsequently informed *Melody Maker*'s Paolo Hewitt, "Step Forward were the only ones to take us on in the beginning. I mean, nobody else would touch us. But (Miles) Copeland was prepared to take the stuff we were doing, like 'Bingo Masters' Breakout' and 'Dragnet' . . . They didn't blink an eye about 'Dragnet'."

The Fall's association with Step Forward lasted approximately 18 months, during which time they released four singles and two albums. It was a relationship based largely on trust: the band weren't signed up in the traditional sense, and neither were Step Forward under any obligation to issue any records for them. When the group wished to do so, an arrangement would be reached whereby the label would press, package and distribute the record on terms that were mutually agreeable. In addition, and of great importance to the band, The Fall were given total control over their press releases and sleeve artwork.

PAINTWORK **CALL YOURSELVES BLOODY PROFESSIONALS?**

Mark Smith, Lyceum, August 1978

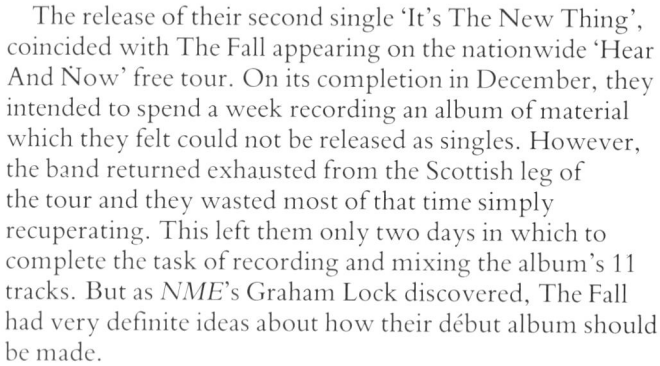

The release of their second single 'It's The New Thing', coincided with The Fall appearing on the nationwide 'Hear And Now' free tour. On its completion in December, they intended to spend a week recording an album of material which they felt could not be released as singles. However, the band returned exhausted from the Scottish leg of the tour and they wasted most of that time simply recuperating. This left them only two days in which to complete the task of recording and mixing the album's 11 tracks. But as *NME*'s Graham Lock discovered, The Fall had very definite ideas about how their début album should be made.

"We tried to do a track in one or two takes," said Smith. "If you do more, people begin to speed up just to get through it, and that's not good for our band because we're not disciplined musicians."

The band were also of the view that production quality was irrelevant. They only enlisted the help of producer Bob Sargeant so that they wouldn't be at the mercy of the engineers.

'Live At The Witch Trials', released in March 1979, enjoyed rapid sales and received favourable reviews. It was perhaps most widely quoted for Smith's (in)famous proclamation, 'We are The Fall, the white crap that talks back!' in 'Crap Rap 2', a thread which reappeared as The Prole Art Threat. Equally, the album's title track, a monologue devoid of customary coyness, caused many a double-take: 'I still believe in the r'n'r dream, r'n'r as primal spirit . . .'

Smith regretted doing it: "It came over more serious than I thought it would. But it's true. I still believe in a kind of purity, that we come from a long line of people who've

PAGE **18**

tried to do things like that – like Gene Vincent – people who were in rock 'n' roll and doing it well, but whose attitude was different."

The songs contained in 'Live At The Witch Trials' were disparate in their focus, each song seemingly a collection of non-sequiturs. As Bramah asked Smith at the start of 'Mother-Sister', 'What's this song about?' – 'Er, nothing,' came the reply. Yet 'Industrial Estate', 'Rebellious Jukebox', and 'Frightened', not to mention the self-explanatory 'Music Scene', all contained germs of many of The Fall's recurring themes: realism, surrealism and paranoia. Sex was conspicuous by its absence, though its earthbound aspects were touched on in later works. On the other hand, the subject of drugs, rock's more iniquitous pastime, was tackled most comprehensively. On this album it appeared in its three guises: the good ('Like To Blow'); the bad ('Underground Medicin'); and more importantly, the ugly ('No Xmas For John Quays') – 'Well, the powders reach, and the powders teach, and when you find that they can reach, then there is no Christmas for John Quays . . . and no girls, no girls, just the traffic passing by, bye-bye, bye-bye . . .'

"'No Xmas For John Quays' is about takers," Graham Lock was told. "It's anti-drugs in a lot of ways. A lot of people use drugs for getting off on and they're mind-fuckers, fucking their own brains. ('He thinks he is more interesting than the world'.) And they really try and get your sympathy, saying, 'Oh, I must have some barbs' – or whatever. And there was this guy – not called John Quays – who just kept wanting things. It was about him really. He was a real bastard."

Martin Bramah, in the same interview, took a more personal approach to the drugs question (as related to The Fall).

"I take drugs," he confessed, "but I don't need it – I don't need to get high. It's like a holiday occasion. But it's definitely where the music comes from . . . I heard our album on acid and it really took off. It didn't sound deadpan or anything."

"I'd prefer to call ours 'head music with energy'," concluded a censorious Mark Smith.

Meanwhile, The Fall, having signed off the dole the previous Christmas, hunkered down to the serious business of earning a living. They toured and recorded almost non-stop throughout 1979, and by the year's end they had crossed the Atlantic. To the outside world it seemed as if The Fall had made it: records that sold well, good turn-outs at their gigs and critical acclaim. But they were existing only on a subsistence level, paying themselves a paltry £10 a week. The Fall on the road, a total of just nine people including the group themselves, bore more resemblance to

PAINTWORK **CALL YOURSELVES BLOODY PROFESSIONALS?**

a 19th Century medicine show than a cult rock band on tour. Mark Smith complained that they had no driver and for roadies they had to rely on the help and good will of a couple of friends.

Besides this financial insecurity, the band were also dogged by numerous personnel changes. Out went drummer Karl Burns early in the New Year, to be replaced by Mike Leigh. A second vacancy, created by Martin Bramah's departure after Easter, was filled from within the band as Marc Riley transferred to guitar, Irishman Steve Hanley now picking up on bass. The Fall had also conscripted a second guitarist, Craig Scanlon, which allowed Riley to moonlight on electric piano when Yvonne Pawlett left after the recording of 'Rowche Rumble' in June. Occasionally Smith would tamper abstractedly with the keyboards, but melody was strictly Riley's domain.

This succession of upheavals, and any discontinuity that may have resulted, was overcome by the band gigging frequently. Some of their London dates saw The Fall in tight, defensive formation as they were brought into contact with the dreaded Apollo/Odeon/Top Rank/Mecca Ballroom leisure industry circuit. This was a kind of latter-day 'Grand Tour' undertaken by record company prodigies. Here they would meet all the other hamsters running round the big wheel . . . "I don't envy those ska bands," observed Smith, "because in three years time . . ."

Martin Bramah, Yvonne Pawlett, Marc Riley, Mark Smith, Karl Burns – August 1978

Martin Bramah, Karl Burns, Mark Smith, Yvonne Pawlett, Marc Riley – August 1978

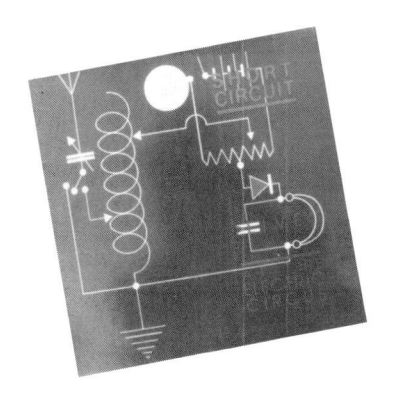

Not surprisingly, it proved to be an anathema to The Fall. When they supported Generation X at the cavernous Lyceum, it was the first time they felt that they were performing just for the money. The reception they got didn't help, either.

"We were getting all those cans," scowled Smith, "and we just thought, 'Let's do our half an hour and piss off,' which is what a lot of bands do all the time."

The Fall certainly showed no such cynicism back home in the north of England. They revelled in the predominant working men's and social club venues (in some towns the only stage for live entertainment), frequently performing in front of unsympathetic audiences. "But we never liked preaching – to the converted, anyway," the band's alter-ego, Roman Totale, declared on the rear of the live LP 'Totale's Turns'. Recorded in exotic Doncaster, Bradford and Preston, 'Totale's Turns' (sub-titled 'It's Now Or Never') was, as Totale himself stated, "Probably the most accurate document of The Fall ever released, even though they'll have a hard time convincing their mams and dads about that, ha ha."

Performing before a dissenting audience made the group's job more difficult, but they weren't out to cosset themselves with select audiences or nurture a brigade of clones. Either side of The Pennines, — The Fall would take to the stage as a bunch of crumpled and outwardly unlikeable malcontents. "Get yer suits off, get yer jeans on!" Smith would yell: The Fall were not to be mistaken for social workers with guitars. This band may have expounded unpalatable faiths and often appeared arrogant, but they were never possessed by vanity or deceit. They can hardly have won many hearts with songs like 'Mess Of My (Age)': 'A mess of our age, a mess of my taste, a mess of our nervous systems – fill the rest in yourself . . . !'

PAGE **21**

PAINTWORK CALL YOURSELVES BLOODY PROFESSIONALS?

Mark Smith, L · S · E –
November 1979

The Fall smeared their fingers in the dirt and showed the locals, 'This is how it is'. They offered the populace no solace, save a cheap night out away from the television. Their songs contained no notions of a promised land, just beer and cigs substituting for milk and honey. Wisely, The Fall left the sweat, the sociology and the unworkable solutions to The Jam, Crass, UB40 and a host of also-rans ("This song's about a retired pit pony . . .")

"The Fall have never played at 'realism'," commented *NME*'s Barney Hoskyns, "but a Fall concert is still a totally political event. Instead of singing about, The Fall dramatise, spin yarns, sing nonsense: a free play of cultural contradictions. Their trash aesthetic does not come from pop culture, because their trash is not disposable, it's everywh re, in false nostalgia, inverted snobbery, puritanism, and in the deadening rituals of boozing, betting and boffing. Smith has collected his trash and treated it with a violent and discomforting humour. Rarely is one treated to such an involved vision. Rare enough are the visionaries, to be sure."

Mark Smith L · S · E –
November 1979

Despite their impeccable working-class credentials and genuine broad accents, The Fall never subscribed to the 'more working-class than thou' vogue prevalent at the turn of the decade. The usual outbursts of dogma, which saw most 'political' bands pinned down under their own cross-fire, were absent from Mark Smith's invective.

"But there again," he interrupted, "nuking Russia might not be a bad idea as far as the bleedin' world's concerned. They've plunged a lot of people into miserable lives. You've only got to go to East Germany to see it – it's horrible, a horrible way to live. It's like Middlesborough."

Neither did Smith have just one string to his bow. Hence The Fall became ever more curious around the time many were shaking their heads in disappointment as The Clash started singing about Cadillacs.

In a way it was quite surprising that The Fall weren't an overtly political band. Of their founder members, Una Baines was a feminist, Tony Friel had flirted with Communism, and Mark Smith himself, though quickly disillusioned, confessed to a heavy involvement in politics

PAINTWORK **CALL YOURSELVES BLOODY PROFESSIONALS?**

Martin Bramah, Mike Leigh, Marc Riley, Yvonne Pawlett, Mark Smith – London, March 1979

before the band. Since The Fall's advent, Smith's disillusionment had turned to disgust. When the band first started up and they had no agent, the laudable Rock Against Racism organisation had lined up several gigs – on the proviso that spokesman Smith held up polemical posters and made announcements between songs.

"They saw you as an entertainment," scorned Smith. "You might as well have been singing Country and Western. And there were Socialist Workers Party workers walking around with leather fists – that's the alternative?"

Smith's political awareness manifested itself in two ways (a chip for each shoulder). Firstly, he succumbed to wrong-headed bigotries (students, white Rastas, the middle class). This was why Fall characters tended at best to get an unfair hearing. Secondly, and more articulately, it expressed itself as fatalism and satire. In a world steeped in irony, the subjects of Smith's songs found themselves cursed, not 'oppressed'. They suffered the injustices of circumstance and not at the hands of their fellow men. For Smith, his fellow man simply played a more active role in the hostile environment.

This obliqueness, later honed into a cryptic house style, was an enormous part of The Fall's appeal, a fact that distressed many critics. Here in their midst was a band that super-abounded in evocative material, but lacked 'Fight war, not wars!' slogans (courtesy of the Crass commune), not to mention the requisite left-field stance. Ergo the band

PAGE 24

must be vague and directionless. As it was their brief to get a handle on The Fall, writers chose to side-step Smith's wry observations in a vain search for something less obvious, a definitive cause. They usually had to settle for an 'angle'. Still, the group appeared to have earned the luxury of their own pigeon-hole.

Other popular misreadings of the band included those who hastily filed them under 'wacky', along with Devo and Human League, simply because of zany titles like 'How I Wrote Elastic Man' and 'Bingo Master's Breakout'. Then there were others who dourly refused to recognise The Fall's capacious sense of humour, as they stuck religiously to the rock journalist's code: 'There is no middle ground!' There's no denying that The Fall should have been taken seriously, but not joylessly so. A library of Smith's couplets attested to this.

Rambling nicely through 'Cash 'n' Carry' on their second John Peel Show appearance, Smith broke off in mid-rant with, 'Oh dear, friends, I can't continue this: Arthur Askey's just been shot!' – Choruses of 'Oh my God!' from the band – 'We'll have to do a tribute, let's do 'Hassle Schmuck'. . . '

It was the age old problem of trying to get one neat label on something as irregular and multi-faceted as The Fall, compounded by a dumb refusal to accept that they were a healthy mess of contradictions: wit, nerve, insight, sourness, awe, paranoia, pride and ignorance. Which was a pretty fair resumé of the human condition.

Evidently, The Fall were out on a limb, out in the wastes. Journalists struggled to keep pace and 'lumpenrocker' contemporaries were abandoned to their fates as Smith and his associates held the seance of 'Dragnet', the band's second album.

'Is there anybody there?' – 'Yeah!'

The invitation was to join The Fall in their 'Psykick Dancehall' ('Get aboard, for ESP medium discord'). New, but not wholly unexpected forces, were now at work in The Fall camp. That Smith had taken a shining to the supernatural was clear in 'Spectre Vs Rector', the first of his brilliant wave of 'short stories': Lost in the fog, a police inspector paid a visit to his friend the rector who, being possessed, attacked him. The inspector, too, was no match for the spectre. Both were saved and the spectre exorcised when on to the scene came a strange hero, 'his soul possessed a thousand times . . .'

'Spectre Vs Rector' derived its power from images created by words and not, as with posturing gothics like Bauhaus, on vocal affectation. Similarly, the acoustic cacophony 'Spectre Vs Rector' had for accompaniment, served its purpose better than any synthesized 'atmospherics'.

The Fall, The Capital, March 1979

Marc Riley, Mark Smith & Steve Hanley, Manchester, July 1979

To have heard The Fall come out with a song like this was like finding a poltergeist in your brand new Bovis home. You'd always had a bad feeling about the place, but as long as the hi-fi and the coffee table stayed put, the presence was perhaps best left undisturbed. It was bound to make itself known sooner or later . . . As for Bauhaus records, they were about as convincing as a ghost train.

Smith began increasingly to cite influences beyond the boundaries of popular culture. Luke Reinhart's book *The Dice Man* surfaced in bastardised form, and the names of Arthur Machen, M.R. James and H.P. Lovecraft, authors of the supernatural, were heard in connection with 'Dragnet'. The phantasmagoric 'A Figure Walks' – "written during a long walk home wearing an anorak which restricted vision by two-thirds" – Smith described as "my Stephen King outing".

Smith's involvement with the immaterial world extended to sightings of ghosts, a belief in reincarnation and the reading of Tarot cards. Kay Carroll, The Fall's manager and true believer, shared Smith's interest in Tarot, but not wishing to appear cranky both had decided to keep it quiet: "Well, you never know when to say it to people because they think you're nutty."

Eventually, Smith stopped giving readings. "I found that when I was doing readings for other people," he told *Record*

Mirror's Nancy Culp, "all my views on the person would come out. Which is how psychics end up, they end up venting all their personal feelings on people . . . This is why I can handle fans really well. There's no problem, because it's easy compared to reading Tarot."

For the most part, The Fall's second LP fell on either deaf or covered ears. Many couldn't hear anything but the awful production and bouts of indulgence. *Melody Maker*'s Paolo Hewitt took even greater exception to it.

"I've played 'Dragnet' not more than four times," he wrote. "And even in the course of duty, couldn't drag myself to it again. To me it's inaccessible, sometimes ugly music, which maybe upsets my world too much, but doesn't help it. After 'Dragnet' I'm not inspired to let The Fall influence my life in any way, but I can admire the spirit behind it."

This spirit was crystallized in a line from 'Choc-Stock', where Smith screeched, 'Let's get this thing together and make it bad!' The song, like 'Dragnet' itself, was a reaction to the scrubbed productions and mellowing attitudes of bands now on to their critical second album. The Clash stumbled with 'Give 'Em Enough Rope', as did Buzzcocks with 'Love Bites' and The Stranglers with 'No More Heroes'; Lord knows how many bit the dust. Some ventured that The Fall came pretty close themselves.

The Fall had been intent on dragging pop bodily into the mire, but it was too little too late. They now stood helplessly by as bands busily hosed down their acts in anticipation of the glamorous and accessible eighties. It seemed that 'Dragnet', as radical an alternative in its way as Public Image Limited's 'Metal Box', was likewise destined to be ignored. Those that did recognise it as a signpost were warned off by the legend: 'This way lies obscurity.'

Steve Hanley & Marc Riley – London School of Economics, November 1979

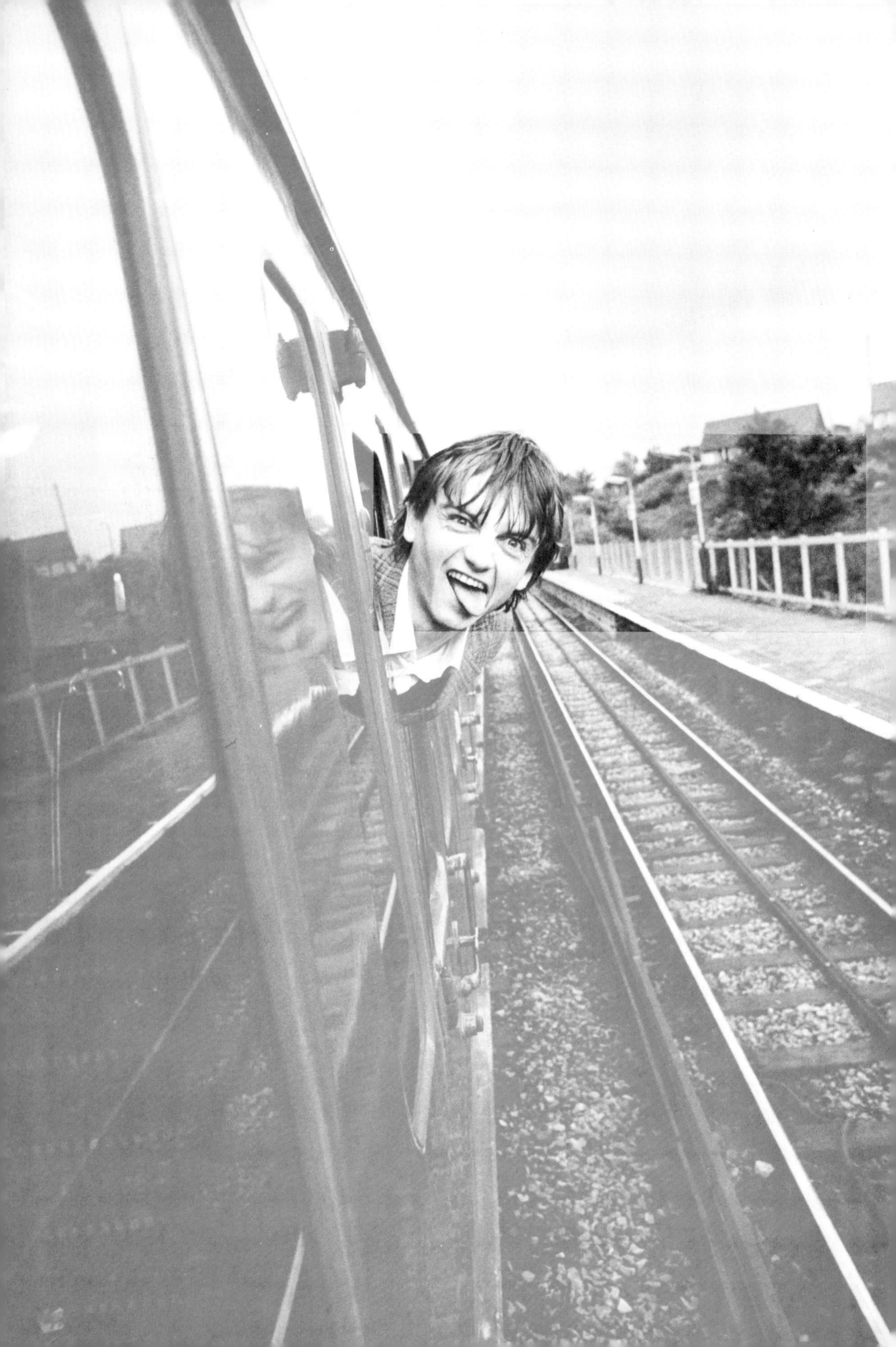

'A spotty exterior hides a spotty interior.' –
'The N.W.R.A.'

CHAPTER 3
ROCK AND POP FILTH

After the havoc of 'Dragnet', everyone breathed a sigh of relief at the appearance of the single 'Fiery Jack'. It was the band's final release on Step Forward, a sprightly, infectious gem that immediately found favour with punters and pundits alike. Quite unexpectedly it seemed as if the band had fulfilled their promise: they proved that The Fall weren't always such hard work, and now everyone was dancing to a strange single about a wild wino whose thought processes (and kidneys) were cauterized by the demon drink . . .

"The first record that stung me into realising how good The Fall could be was 'Fiery Jack'," enthused *NME* writer Andy Gill. "A spiky but streamlined slice of eighties urban rockabilly which knocks the spots off the retrogressive, style-orientated offerings of such as The Polecats."

Sadly, 'Fiery Jack' also marked the demise of Roman Totale. The Mythos ended with the discovery in the remote Welsh hills of a statement – and a master-tape – alongside the last remains of R. Totale. Part of that statement read, "I have not long left now but I urge the finder of this 'master-tape' never to unleash it on humanity!"

The single was released and Totale, by now bearing all the hallmarks of a laboured in-joke, was killed off. Mark Smith no longer had time for games, nor had the band any further need of an organ of self-criticism. 'Vicious son' Joe Totale inherited some of his father's duties, but none of his trusting nature. For a while he appeared on hand-outs at gigs and briefly held a position of responsibility writing damning sleeve notes for The Fall. He probably emigrated.

The Fall, meanwhile, had pulled off a coup. Breaking out of the cosy English scene the band took the sideways step to play in America. This challenge was realised with the help of Step Forward before the band had decided to shack up with leading independents Rough Trade early in 1980. While over there The Fall encountered, as described in 'Cash 'n' Carry', 'English groups, acting like peasants with free milk, on a route to the loot, to candy mountain . . .'

A contemptuous Mark Smith related the experience to *Melody Maker*'s Paolo Hewitt. "We got over to Los Angeles," he sneered, "and all the people there hate the English bands, because they come over and they're just like The Climax Blues Band. It's the same trip. They do the big halls, loads of money, come on and play two hour sets with solos. I mean, the new wave bands I saw . . . ! You can imagine, the Virgin new wave bands go over there and they

Opposite: En route to Manchester, May 1980

get into the cocaine and they're playing to all those fat, coked-up idiots in big halls who just want to hear guitars loud."

Despite the brevity of the visit – a dozen dates, mainly on the West Coast – it gave The Fall a necessary perspective on Britain's overcrowded scene, where the genuine talent was being engulfed in a flash flood of benign, guitar-wielding misfits. Even the creative loopholes were fast closing up, or as Smith put it . . . "The conventional is now experimental." With this new wave of indiscriminate acceptance, the once indigestible music of Cabaret Voltaire and Throbbing Gristle was happily consumed along with everything else.

This knowledge, combined with their recent American experiences, made the band realise how important it was not to become complacent in these cushy times. So they got tough: Smith with the band, and the band with the audience. Smith, already known for being a 'little Hitler', became even more dictatorial with his musicians. On the live version of 'No Xmas For John Quays' on 'Totale's Turns' he could be heard encouraging them to 'put some fucking guts into it, for Christ's sake!'

Smith defended the hard line he was taking. "If you want to create something," he told *Sounds*' Edwin Pouncey, "if you're going to do music, you've got to have a bit of discipline about it, because without discipline it's just a morass of rubbish."

The Fall's attitude to audiences also went against the grain. Instead of pandering to appreciative crowds, they dragged them up by their lapels, slapped them about a bit, and disorientated them still further by dropping even more old material than was their normal habit. Within nine months of 'Fiery Jack' winning over thousands to their cause, The Fall dropped it from their sets.

"We could go out with a set of stuff we've recorded and go down a storm," said Smith, taking a swipe at the likes of Stiff Little Fingers. "But we don't want to do that. Nobody's got the right to lay that on us. Every band does it and it's the death of every band."

The Fall also set to work pruning their established audience by alienating certain sections, namely the punks, the so-called 'raincoat and carrier bag brigade', and as many students as they could lay their hands on. Smith could not abide the thought of The Fall being regarded as any one clique's particular property. Punks were reviled on the basis that they viewed the band as part of 'the 1977 thing', besides which they persisted with the once-fashionable pastime of spitting. His reaction to being used as a target was immortalised on 'Totale's Turns'.

'Are you doing what you did two years ago?' Smith raged, at some poor sod stupid enough to gob at him.

Mark Smith, London, February 1980

'Yeah? Well don't make a career out of it!'

The 'raincoats' were too precious, too safe, too removed from The Fall's grubby reality. The further education fraternity were cold-shouldered because of conventions of non-conformism – three years of dope, dyed hair and earrings. Not that our hero had ever forgotten how students' union officials had refused him entry to a Can gig at Manchester University when he was 16 on the grounds that he wasn't a student. From the outset he vowed that The Fall would operate a policy of not playing at universities or colleges where student-only concerts were held.

Such was Smith's dislike of these august seats of learning that he steered clear of Factory Records because they were on the other side of Manchester . . . "y'know, the University side."

What kind of audience The Fall were actually after remained a mystery; perhaps one that could make up its own mind, have a few beers and behave itself. "A good comedian's audience," offered Smith. Anyway, attendances didn't dwindle for all that, though audiences became noticeably polarised. The band's music, or more accurately, the attitude behind and the delivery of that music forced the listener to take sides: a simple choice if you didn't like being harangued one minute and ignored the next. As far as the group were concerned, you were either for or agin' The Fall. Indifference was not countenanced.

"All five look disinterested, but perversely normal," noted Paolo Hewitt at a North London Poly gig. "They are not playing pop star games for the audience. Only their music. They don't look for adoration or applause. Just a reaction. Which they are getting . . . Not up front where their fans are clustered, uncritical of their every move, but towards the back where people shift uneasily, unable to look away, standing next to others who are either heading for the understaffed bar complaining of the 'racket' they make, or shouting abuse."

"Their music isn't difficult to listen to," concurred *NME*'s Graham Lock. "What throws the audience is the group's refusal to use any of the customary tactics of presentation. They employ no charisma, no charm, no theatricality. They don't even pretend to have fun. And they neglect to regurgitate old crowd-pleasers." At this time, Mark Smith had also adopted the endearing quality of slagging off other bands in the press, the object of his disgust being The Great Escape. Recently, there had been a disturbing drift towards the immaculately-coiffured, fast entertainment business where, with a good agent and an even better stylist, you stood a fair chance of getting on *Top Of The Pops*. Liking what they saw, fashionable types

Mark Smith, London, August 1981

PAINTWORK **ROCK AND POP FILTH**

Mark Smith, Manchester, May 1980

flooded out of the closet, tried on the music for size and found that it fitted. "All fashions are filched off faggots!" declared Smith.

To cut a long story short, the staunchly anti-escapist Fall were wholly against this idea of pursuing the pose of the hour. Smith railed against journalistic fashion-mongers, who were promoting the importance of, if you please, 'looking good when the bomb drops'. This came out in a number of music press interviews, not to mention the song 'Look, Know': 'He was the first one to wear a flying jacket and go to a club, and she has a policy of not being seen dead in a pub . . . '

The cover of 'Look, Know' also bore the wry by-line, 'You know it needs a lens'. Smith's puritanism, or more precisely his 'righteous maelstrom', duly led to him being labelled 'the stroppiest sod this side of Johnny Rotten'. Still, having acquired the reputation, among music journalists especially, of being a 'difficult bastard', Smith saw no reason to play this down, though nearly all commented on how accommodating he was in interviews. And above all he was outspoken, a trait very much in keeping with Smith's abhorrence of spiritual and physical laziness which, as he told *NME*'s Andy Gill . . . "is typical of the 'rock' sort of thing today."

For a good few years Mark Smith remained one of the most widely quoted figures in the music business. When not acting as rock's outraged conscience, a title he loathed but a role that fitted him like a glove, he could always be relied upon to give another instalment of his 'Unpopular Opinions In Populist Times'. "I want to be didactic," Smith stressed. "I want to be opinionated. I don't think because we're having a fucking hard time everybody should stop having opinions and start getting into good-time stuff. I think people in hard times need brain stimulation more than at any time."

At the hour of The Fall's departure from Step Forward, Smith dared mention the filthy lucre in saying that the band had had the thin end of the wedge for too long. Step Forward ought to have rumbled this discontent from 'Before The Moon Falls' on 'Dragnet', containing as it did the telling line, 'I could use some pure criminals to get my hands on some royalties . . .'

"They were so into action all the time," added Smith, "that we found we were being left behind. And with a band like us we need some kind of security because we don't operate on those lines. The other bands they had, like Squeeze and The Police, it was okay for them because one day they were going to get signed up. But we didn't particularly want to be A&M trailers, and we were skint all the time."

It sounded like sour grapes, but Smith only had the group's best interests at heart. Like many groups that

Steve Hanley, Craig Scanlon, Marc Riley, Mike Hee & Mark Smith

weren't 'signed up', The Fall in their turn (ripe for the dragnet) had received overtures from major companies. These were turned down as being 'sub-standard'. "The record companies that do approach you are usually the shoddy ones," maintained Smith.

In the event, the band pitched in with Rough Trade, a pokey Notting Hill record shop turned record label whose popularity and influence had ballooned since punk's Big Bang. At the time, the band were impressed with this small, self-contained outlet, which boasted its own distribution network. Rough Trade was one of a very small number of independent labels able to reach the expanding alternative market every bit as well as the chain stores. However, this relationship, too, was destined to turn sour.

It began promisingly enough in April with 'Totale's Turns'. Critic Andy Gill later said he had . . . "come to regard it as the best – and most honest – live album of 1980. Its superficially shoddy exterior hides a heart of hardened self-respect, which more than makes up for any shortcomings in the area of recording."

Hot on its heels came 'How I Wrote Elastic Man', released in July 1980, followed barely two months later by 'Totally Wired'. Together they reinforced the off-beat, up-tempo impact of 'Fiery Jack'. Eminent Fall-o-phile John Peel was much taken with 'Totally Wired', identifying strongly with the lines, 'you don't have to be weird to be weird – you don't have to be strange to be strange.' He literally demanded its inclusion on Radio One's *Roundtable* playlist, come his turn to appear on the new releases forum. (Legend also had it that Rod Stewart used 'Totally Wired' as an intro to his shows.) The popular number 'Container Drivers', later recorded for a Peel Session, completed a quartet of songs that temporarily earned the band a simplistic 'northern rockabilly' tag.

Having Peel's backing was as good as royal patronage, but this didn't prevent The Fall from promoting their records during sessions recorded for his late-night show. 'Live At The Witch Trials' had been pushed during a suitably quiet moment in 'No Xmas For John Quays', with Smith slipping in the ad-lib, 'Make sure the album this song is on is in your Christmas stocking!' Similarly, as an introduction to 'New Face In Hell' the words 'This is off the new LP!', cheekily heralded the arrival of 'Grotesque', the group's third and strongest studio album to date.

'Grotesque (After The Gramme)' appeared in the shops in November 1980. It underlined both The Fall's musical confidence and Smith's growing lyrical maturity, as recently witnessed in 'Totally Wired'. *Sounds*' writer Edwin Pouncey, correcting a widely-held belief that The Fall were a ramshackle bunch of bedlamites, offered that their music was anything but loud and disorderly. "The whole Fall

Mark Smith, Marc Riley, Steve Hanley, Paul Hanley, Craig Scanlon – Manchester, May 1980

sound is not, as some seem to think, a musical kickabout but structured and complete," he stated. "The Fall are a rhythm section tight and disciplined, a well-tuned dance machine in the truest sense of the word dance, a firm foundation created to give Mark the freedom to let fly. With such a band behind him he can get on and do what he feels he must do without worry. It is their strength that provides the empty canvas for Mark to paint his pictures of words."

'O'er grassy dale and lowland scene, come see, come hear the English Scheme . . .': this was the phoney setting for 'Grotesque'. Behind lay the most vivid Fall imagery – bad housing, 'grotesque peasants', shells of churches, darkness, successful wretches, ugliness, monsters, strangeness – fantasy and reality congealed in a jar. The album's 'short-stories', 'New Face In Hell' ('Wireless enthusiast intercepts government secret radio band and uncovers secrets and scandals of deceitful-type proportions . . .') and 'Impression Of J. Temperance', a tale about an unlikeable character whose mutant offspring was 'fed with rubbish from disposal barges . . .', were pure Fall.

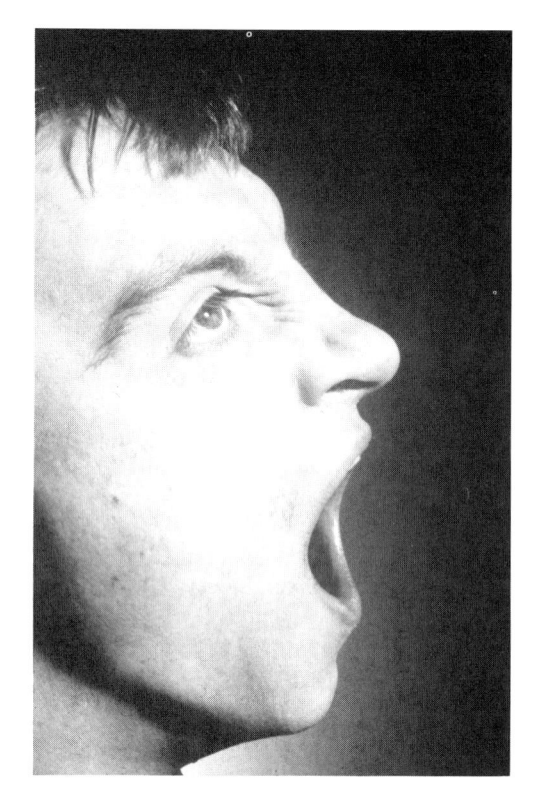

It was no exaggeration to say that in The Fall's hands fiction became rumoured fact. There was a strong possibility that these things actually happened in some grim corner of the country. Perhaps only Nick Cave, in league with The Birthday Party and later The Bad Seeds, has since held a (guttering) candle to Smith's unique excursions into the twilight.

The songs on 'Grotesque' were hard-hitting and clear. They communicated where the occasional unpoetic clutter of 'Witch Trials' and 'Dragnet' had partly obscured. Smith now executed his ideas without hesitation, as if he had suddenly come to understand the power of his own words. The familiar lyrical barrage appeared totally bereft of pretension, indulgence, and waste. Hence the imagery of 'Hydrochloric shaved weirds', 'Five wacky English proletariat idiots' and 'I am Robinson Speed and this is my Gramme Friday' made immediate contact with the listener.

Smith had been less impressed by people mistaking 'The North Will Rise Again' as 'another provincialist rant', a comment about the north-south divide. "It was the fucking centrepiece of the album, for me. I really worked on that. And I thought people would take it a bit less on face value." Mark Smith explained to Andy Gill that it, too, was a story, a concept along the lines of 'Nazis Invade Britain', and not some kind of political statement. (There were some who chose to read 'NWRA', as it appeared on the LP, as North West Republican Army . . .)

"The way I wrote it was from a few dreams I had after playing up north a lot," revealed Smith. "It's about what would happen if there were a revolution. It's purely fantasy, sci-fi stuff. ('When it happens we'll walk through the estates from Manchester right up to Newcastle'.) But of course everybody's going, 'Huh! the north! Here we go again – Smith talking about flat caps and flat beer,' and all that clichéd rubbish. Actually, the message is that if the north did rise again, they would fuck it up. Not that they ever rose before . . . " And Smith narrated: 'The streets of Soho did reverberate with drunken Highland men, revenge for Culloden dead: the north had rose again.'

The irony of course, was that there were riots in Toxteth and Moss Side the following year. And The Fall were on a seven-week tour of America at the time. In Atlanta, Georgia, to be precise, where Mark Smith glimpsed a passer-by's newspaper. On reading the headlines Smith recalled thinking, "Christ! The north has risen at last and here's me sitting in Atlanta! – So I ran out to find the nearest paper shop, but in America it was, like, six miles away . . ."

Returning to England, as he told *Sounds*' reporter Mick Middles, Smith found it was as he'd descrbed it in 'English Scheme': 'Start the revolution when the pubs shut.'

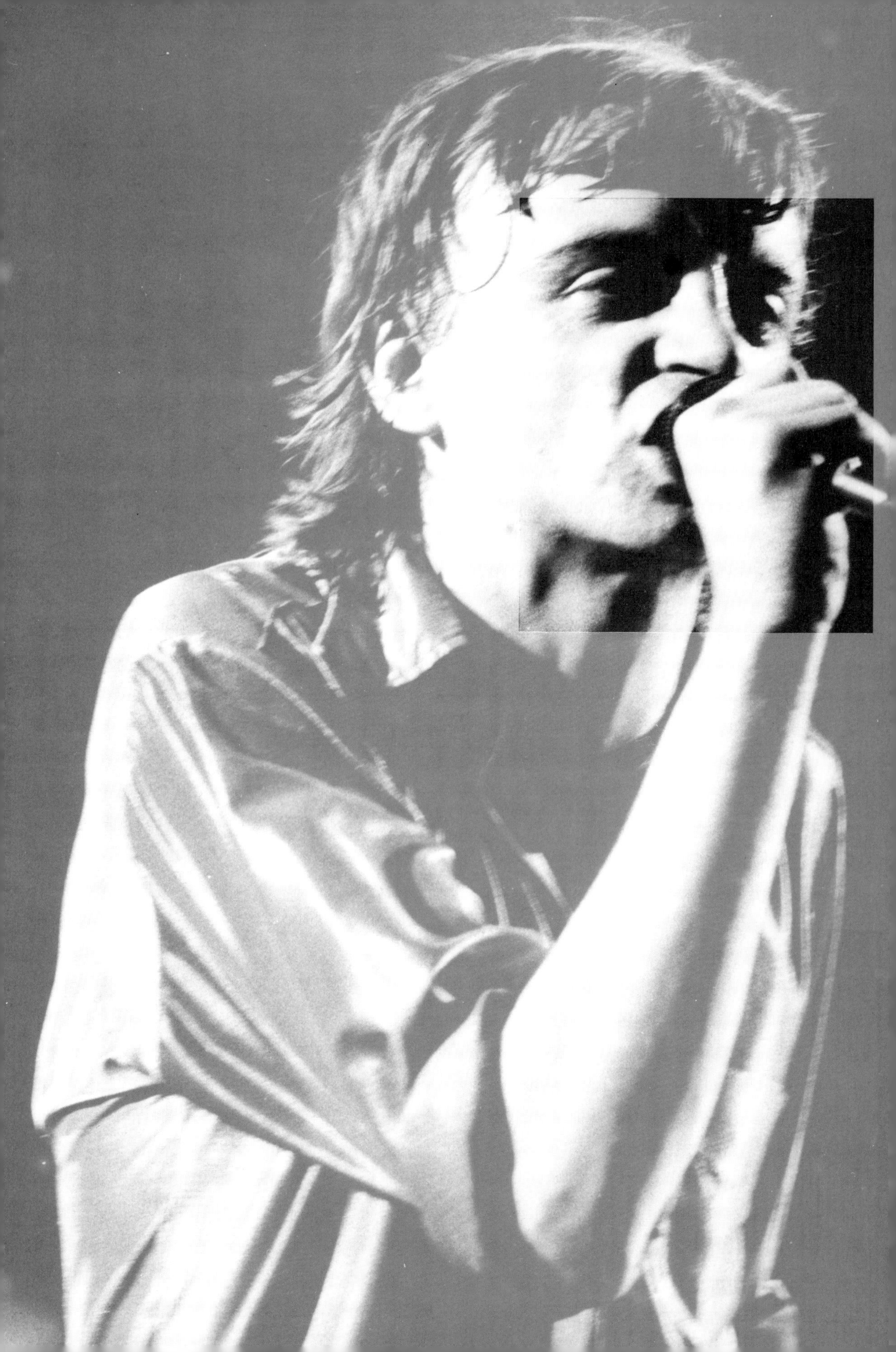

'He learned a word today, the word's 'misanthropy'.' –
'Middle Mass'.

CHAPTER 4
PROLE ART THEATRE /SCHISM

The 1981 American tour thoroughly agreed with The Fall: the experience neither dwarfed them nor inspired them to smash up hotel rooms. Far from playing at bored rock-stars, The Fall took pride in having financed the trip themselves and heartily enjoyed the challenge of taking their scurvy music to untouched audiences.

"We played places where they hadn't had a band for 10 years," Smith enthused to *NME*'s Barney Hoskyns. "Those kids in the Mid-West have got no preconceptions, so you're taken on your true worth. We got a lot of catcalls, but it was like starting all over again, it was great."

The band had also relished New World grotesqueness, sights even more peculiar than the gaunt figure of Mark Smith hunched over a microphone, singing about Kwik Save, Wigan Casino and duffle coats in front of an American audience. They'd seen the sights of San Francisco, Las Vegas, New York, and in Memphis, Tennessee, The Fall filed through the tacky 'theme rooms' of Graceland, Mecca for Elvis Presley worshippers the world over. Mark Smith, however, held a greater admiration for The King's musical roots, Sun Records, the studio where it really all began.

"Those innovators are still there," reflected Smith, "and nobody's heard of them. And Sun Records sits, like, between a garage and a porn shop and you hardly notice it . . ."

Subsequent interviews with The Fall were full of recollections of "businessmen in Hawaiian shirts" and the strange set-up of your typical American venue. Marc Riley told *NME* writer Andy Gill of the time they supported Iggy Pop.

"It was a big 'Talk Of The Town' or something," beamed Riley. "There were all these couples sat round tables, drinking wine, and just a couple of people stood there at the front looking at us. Really weird! Like a cabaret really . . . They treat their music differently from the way we do – it's like the pictures there, like going to see a movie. They eat and everything while you're on: they're sat there and you're going wild, y'know?"

All very unnatural. Which was what shocked promoters thought of the weirdo set attracted by The Fall. Mark Smith recalled the band going down particularly well with the LA underground: "Managers of halls would say, 'God, we've never had any junkies in the audience before, we've never had any whores . . . ' "

As with their previous American trip, The Fall inevitably bumped into other English bands doing the rounds. Turned off by their compatriots' willingness to adopt exaggerated Englishness for the American market – the patronising street-wise stances, phoney cockney accents and stage-costume bondage trousers – they began putting down the UK alternative scene. They also had a hard time convincing bands from across the water that the American record-buying public were consumers first and foremost, that their 'instruments of change' were mere stage props over there, tools of a commercialised trade.

This notion that England was exporting something culturally vital was all wind in sails. Place a band like The Clash on a vast stage in a US sports stadium, a routine followed a few years later by U2 and Simple Minds, and the intimacy of a piece like 'White Riot' was lost. With one foot on the monitor, guitar against the hip, the band would unwittingly transform the song into a heavy rock anthem, perhaps mopping up with a bit of good ol' rhythm and blues, the universal language of boogie-woogie.

Mark Smith was of the opinion that in the States, British bands were in any case viewed as . . . "cute skinny limeys who danced around like idiots." Stripped of their myth and stature abroad, The Fall perceived themselves as separate from all of this. On the one hand they were as English as blackberry and apple pie; on the other, their music was almost unpalatably original. Too well laced with popular rock idiom to be branded an oddity, too unconventional to be tossed into the mainstream, The Fall had to be taken on the merit of their demanding, unfamiliar music.

The fact that so many bands were just variations on the 'rock' theme heightened the musical barrenness of 'Winter' and 'An Older Lover', The Fall courageously baring all when they could have easily hidden behind a rapid-fire set of country and northern classics. Their applause was somehow earned, not given out of politeness or frenzy. "Thank you," said Mark Smith, responding to a Chicago crowd's warm appreciation of 'Hip Priest'. "That one usually clears the halls . . . "

Highlights of the 1981 American tour appeared the following year on a live import LP entitled 'A Part Of America Therein', a good quality pressing on the Cottage Records label. The album captured wonderful moments like Marc Riley's comical kazoo intro to 'The N.W.R.A.', the band having been given a heroes' welcome by the Tut Club's MC.

While 'A Part Of America Therein' didn't contain any previously unrecorded material, it was every bit as accurate a document as its predecessors 'Totale's Turns' and Chaos Tapes' recently released cassette 'Live At Acklam Hall, London 1980'. The latter was particularly in keeping with the group's appealingly shabby image. An unpolished recording, complete with out-of-tune backing vocals on 'Jawbone And The Air Rifle' and an incorrect song listing, was exactly what the band were about, faces in someone's 'warts-and-all' scrapbook. Whenever and wherever live tapes appeared, and there have been plenty of unofficial bootlegs, they gave a far greater insight into the current state of The Fall than any music press article, the film, as it were, being more eloquent than its sub-titles.

Apart from this one anomalous appearance, the Chaos Tapes rota was otherwise exclusively hardcore punk – Discharge, Anti Pasti, GBH – emphasizing the fact that The Fall were essentially a live band. Like their unsophisticated labelmates, they too could be cheaply and above all viably produced. The tons of technology shipped in, for example, to chronicle Siouxsie And The Banshees' taming of the Royal Albert Hall, would be wasted on the spangleless Fall.

Of the records produced by The Fall in 1981, including the retrospective 'Fall – The Early Years 1977-79', 'Slates' was far and away the gruffest and most significant. In common with 'Grotesque' it featured the Hanley brothers, Steve and now young drummer Paul, who had replaced Karl Burns. Smith, in one of The Fall's press releases, had optimistically ventured that Paul Hanley, "will one day form the greatest rhythm section ever with his brother." Needless to say, Karl Burns rejoined the group shortly afterwards, appearing on the credits of 'A Part Of America Therein' . . .

Released in April prior to the American tour, the six-track 10-inch disc found a loving home among loyal fans and drew praise from critical circles, praise which had been unforthcoming on 'Grotesque'. Where 'Grotesque' had been lean, 'Slates' was tough. The music was snapped into position and kept in place by Smith's firm hand. 'Don't start improvising, for Christ's sake!' he chided on 'Slates, Slags Etc', as Riley, Hanley and Scanlon itched to deviate from the song's rigid course.

"A lot of alternative bands think you can just go out and do it," Smith said to *NME*'s Richard Cook, "I detest that fuckin' attitude. It's best to sound bad than do the smug improvisation thing. I get sent loads of records full of that sort of thing from people who shouldn't go near a studio." Smith's vocal delivery was cocksure on 'Fit And Working Again'; on 'Middle Mass' it was hissing and insidious ('And living here you whisper, bub . . . '), and on the scathing 'Leave The Capitol' his voice was nothing short of experienced: 'Hotel maids smile in unison, then you know in your brain (chortles) you know in your brain – leave the capital! Exit this Roman shell . . . !' – "Any capital", it said on the sleeve, but the song's gloriously dense text revealed sick, friendly-faced London, the '10 times town'.

Bored with traditional rock dives, the capital's god-makers scanned the provinces for activity. Liverpool and Manchester provided the spoils of previous crusades; now Scotland was shoved half-prepared upon the pedestal. The papers were full of them: Orange Juice, The Associates, Fire Engines. Charming, absolutely charming. The press even set about making puppet kings of labels the way big record companies made *Smash Hits* stars out of one-hit wonders. For a time, Postcard Records was allowed to eclipse even Factory.

New Musical Express, *Sounds*, and to a lesser extent *Melody Maker*, had become slaves to the Marxist/Darwinian change-and-progress kick every bit as much as the *Daily Mail* was now obsessed with a return to Victorian values. And the readers swallowed it chapter and verse. These publications were suddenly full of gushy, well-intentioned pieces about new bands: throw in a bit of reggae, Van Morrison, The Specials and you had what Mark Smith called an 'obligatory cosmopolitan music viewpoint'. Objective reporting flew out of the window.

Similarly, there was now a heavy editorial bias along the anti-racist/anti-sexist/Northern Ireland/CND/mass unemployment axis. Decidedly left of centre, it went unchecked and unquestioned, and listening to and reading about music became very much a consciousness-raising exercise. With 10 bands for every cause, this was to some extent inevitable. The *NME* in particular soon resembled a fanatically-run, over-funded community arts project that commissioned dreadful social realist murals simply because community arts projects *did* commission dreadful social realist murals.

"When I want to read politics," Smith informed *Melody Maker*, "I buy *New Statesman*. It's as simple as that."

'Prole Art Threat', a swipe at this kind of 'knee-jerk liberalism', saw Smith thinly disguising the attack as "a sort of play about a commuter-type bloke who flips out on leftism." The track, like 'Slates' as a whole, reaffirmed that the south was completely lacking in proletarian culture, that the region was geared to fashion and not necessity. The Fall were an embodiment of this realisation, raising two fingers where others kowtowed. As Richard Cook wrote in *NME*, "At a moment when pop has become besotted with its visual trappings, The Fall have made their strongest play for an identity based entirely on sound."

'Prole Art Threat' implied that the north ended up with all the ill-fitting hand-me-downs and suffered as a consequence. The Fall were just part of the pay-off. "Maybe one day," Roman Totale had once dared hope, "a northern sound will emerge not tied to that death circuit attitude or merely reiterating movements based in the capital."

The ascendant skinhead bands, patronised almost solely by *Sounds*' Gary Bushell, were an exception to this divisive rule. Though Mark Smith remained unenamoured by this noisome bunch, he did at least concede to the uncomfortable truth about Oi.

"It's a more honest political statement than anything else going down," he maintained. "I think it's a genuine statement. And it's a lot more convincing than the Gang Of Four will ever be. It says a lot about England, that music."

"And of course these kids think of The Fall as the same as all these other pretentious groups," Smith later told *Sounds*' Sandy Robertson. "And that's why 'Slates' came out as something totally unfathomable, neither an EP nor an LP."

With The Fall at backstreet level, 'Slates' ought to have reached those waylaid by Oi music, but the ciphers were wrong, unidentifiable. The band themselves came to blows with their record company over 'Slates'.

"I was dead proud of 'Slates'," *Sounds*' writer Edwin Pouncey discovered. "And I didn't think it did as well as it could. I thought that record could have been one of the greatest changes in music if it had been pushed right: the format, the subject matter and everything. All Rough Trade could come out with was, 'Oh it's not very nice the way you slag off so and so', and all this bloody crap."

They had encountered similar opposition with the release of 'Totally Wired'. The Fall felt, rightly or wrongly, that the single's potential had never been fully realised, Rough Trade having declined to market it positively. In short, they weren't behind the band, they weren't there when they were needed and this time the band had had enough. The Fall duly walked out.

Mid-summer 1981 saw The Fall in Iceland as unlikely ambassadors of British rock. They were only the fourth such group to have set foot on the nation's volcanic soil in the past three years, and, in the light of this rare event, Reykjavik's leading newspaper was moved to run a front page feature entitled, 'British Raw Rockers Arrive In Iceland'. When you considered that Icelanders are accustomed to flying 900-odd miles to Oslo in Norway to see a gig this headline seems slightly less bizarre. In terms of both scale and setting (the Apollo astronauts had trained in Iceland for their moonwalks), the three-date mini-tour was in stark contrast to their recent trek around The States. *Melody Maker*'s Colin Irwin recorded manager Kay Carroll's first impressions.

"No beer," she moaned. "No trees, no telly on Thursdays or in the whole of July, no cigarettes, and blokes walking round with toilet rolls in their ears – what kind of a place is this?" The final comment concerned officials

PAINTWORK **PROLE ART THEATRE/SCHISM**

monitoring a soundcheck to make sure they weren't exceeding the strictly observed limit of 100 decibels. Nudity, on the other hand, was tolerated, as the group discovered when girls fronting the support act Q4U appeared dressed for the stage of the Paul Raymond Revue Bar.

Live venues being few and far between, The Fall's shows were sell-outs, though the locals didn't always appreciate the merchandise. This usually involved nothing more than staring contests with members of the vodka-crazed audience, but on one occasion Smith had a chair flung at him by a huge, drunken trawlerman. "He only did it because he liked you," observed Kay Carroll.

Drunkenness is commonplace in Iceland. Colin Irwin highlighted this with an incident which saw Mark Smith, to quote the song, 'Fall down flat in the Café Iol, without a glance from the clientèle . . . ' "Mark decided to go for a coffee in the café across the road," wrote Irwin. "He tripped, and tumbled across a pile of tables. Nobody laughed. Nobody got upset. Nobody blinked. They thought he was drunk . . . "

'My life should be full of strangeness,' Smith sang on 'How I Wrote Elastic Man', 'like a rich painting . . . ' Iceland certainly fulfilled this desire. Blame it on the vodka, blame it on the isolation, the desolate landscapes, the legends – this place had all the weirdness and vibrations he could wish for. Not to mention Megas Jonsson, the enigmatic father-figure of Icelandic rock and roll, whom The Fall inevitably ran into. Jonsson lived in enforced retirement, having been ostracised for his blasphemous treatment of The Sagas (akin to sending up Shakespeare, The Church of England and The Royal Family all in one go), and intemperate use of drugs and alcohol. Smith took a shine to the man and his music straight away.

All these events and impressions culminated in 'Iceland', recorded appropriately in a lava-walled Reykjavik studio. It was a subtle example of The Fall's genuine gift for spontaneity.

"Right, no dicking about," announced Smith, "let's get set up – we've wasted enough money already." Having been told they were going to do a new song, the musicians gladly obliged. Drums pattered, Riley plucked notes out of a banjo and Scanlon tripped out the groggy tune on a piano. Over this Smith played a tape of the wind howling at his hotel window, and spoke his fragile lyrics: 'Cast the runes against your own soul, roll up for the underpants show . . . to be humbled in Iceland . . .'

"No, we didn't know what he was going to do either," marvelled Riley. "He just said he needed a tune, something Dylanish, and we knocked around on the piano and came up with that. But we hadn't heard the words until he suddenly did them. We did 'Fit And Working Again' on 'Slates' in exactly the same way. Yeah, I suppose it's amazing really."

Along with their duty frees, The Fall returned to England with Purrkur Pilnikk, who later guested with the band on their 1982 tour.

Back home The Fall kept up the pressure, gigging relentlessly, all the time building up to 'Hex' and winning over audiences with an impressive rhythmic barrage meted out by the group's new two-drum line-up. In full flight nobody could touch them.

"The Fall," wrote *NME*'s Barney Hoskyns, "are playing the most intense, hypnotic rock 'n' roll since The Velvets of 'Sister Ray'; as Marc Riley keeps up a brilliant, fevered Cale organ part, Craig Scanlon batters his guitar, Steve Hanley's bass pins every beat to the floor, and the dual drum unit of Karl Burns and Paul Hanley never lets off its devastating power for nigh on 10 minutes. After five of these, you feel quite simply entranced, ecstatic.

"Smith sauntering about the stage with icily calculated indifference only adds to the sheer rigour of the sound. He addresses nobody, but his delivery is fanatical. Sometimes you can make out his words, at other times not; it doesn't

PAINTWORK **PROLE ART THEATRE/SCHISM**

matter, the challenge to both heart and mind is there."

The Fall were now regularly playing these intense 90-minute sets, Smith driven almost to nervous exhaustion through speed and his appetite for rearranging the sheer mass of new material in readiness for each night's show.

During the period late 1981 to mid-1982, The Fall were at their mightiest, their most inspired. This was their last truly quantum leap: after 'Hex' The Fall always seemed to know what they were doing, to be aware of the fact that they were The Fall. The mistakes they made were small, somehow less endearing, as if they were trying not to make any errors. But this was to criticise. To reach this point had been a feat of endurance that left the likes of Killing Joke and Theatre Of Hate gasping for breath after a couple of plausible singles. The Fall still had one hell of a way to go.

The single 'Lie-Dream Of A Casino Soul', released in November on the obscure Kamera label, was the presage of 'Hex Enduction Hour'. Raucous, tight, even well-produced by Fall standards, it promised excellence and very little mercy. For those unaccustomed to Smith's syntactical mischief and his musicians' creative butchery, there was only one option open: dance or be damned. For those who had grown up with The Fall, this was their finest hour.

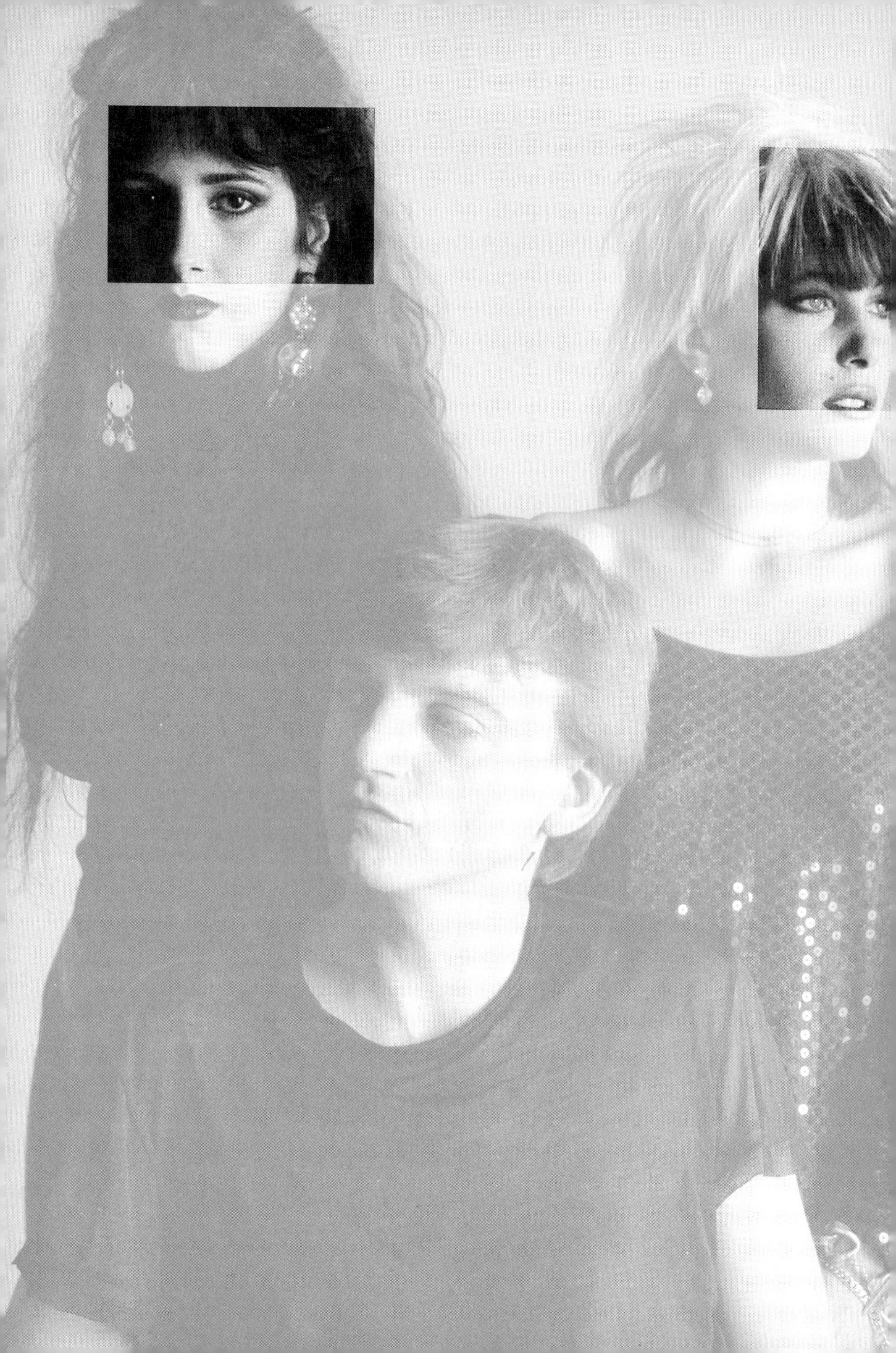

'Make a grab for the book of prayers.' – 'Iceland'.

CHAPTER 5
WORDS OF EXPECTATION

After the magnificent 'Hex Enduction Hour' saw release in the Spring of 1982, The Fall attained 'hot property' status. They now attracted the unwelcome attention of various 'interested parties', which for Mark Smith meant fielding dozens of unsolicited telephone calls, turning down one wonderful offer after another. Ripe cherry that The Fall were, he wasn't about to push them into the pop arena for slick consumption and he had no qualms about disappointing everyone from TV producers to T-shirt manufacturers – "Mere Grubby Pseuds making capital out of The Fall sweat and precognition."

Five years of hard graft and heartache, Smith felt, had earned the band some measure of respect, not a meal ticket for the cockroaches. Releases after this date often bore stern warnings: 'Badge and shirtmakers not reporting to this man will be persecuted to the fullest extent.'

The album was culled partly from the Iceland sessions, with the bulk of the material recorded in Hitchin's disused Regal Cinema. Here the band achieved the desired 'well-produced noise', something very close to their live sound.

"Jangled guitars irritate," observed *Record Mirror*'s Mark Cooper, "and Smith's voice is still mixed down, a whining insinuating voice asserting itself from the back. The voice verges on the unintelligible, has too many words to say, refuses to shape and package its outpourings, remains defiantly cryptic . . . Now The Fall have realised a new and commanding warrior charge, a splash of cymbals, a grumbling bass and a choppy surge of guitars that is capable of delicacy but never of cleanliness. With two drummers and still two guitars, The Fall are now a perfect racket, fiery and untamed."

Predictably, there were others in the trade more hung-up on production quality than artistic merit. "This Swiss guy from Krokus said he could have done a better production on a four-track when he was pissed," said Smith, forlornly. Neither did they win many awards for the cover of 'Hex Enduction Hour'. HMV took such a dislike to its coarse appearance that they would only display the record back to front. The management felt that whereas the sleeve front had about as much to do with design as a toilet wall, the back at least conformed to accepted conventions of layout and typography. Mark Smith offered his perspective to *Sounds*' Sandy Robertson.

"I like the cover to reflect what's inside," he explained, complaining that most albums were all cover and no guts.

"I think rock artwork has gone right down the drain – I do all my own. Like, I love all those misspelt posters – a graphic designer would never get it right in years! My attitude to the sleeve is the same as my attitude to music . . ."

Uncompromising had become a greatly over-used word, but The Fall pulled not a single punch with 'Hex Enduction Hour'. For an entrance, 'The Classical' had all the subtlety of a police raid: 'There is no culture is my brag. Your taste for bullshit reveals a lust for a home of office. This is the home of the vain, this is the home of the vain! Where are the obligatory niggers? Hey there, Fuckface! Hey there, Fuckface!'

Why The Fall were never carpeted for the word 'nigger' was a complete mystery. Joy Division, New Order, and Siouxsie And The Banshees were all clapped in irons at one time or another for alleged anti-semitism. Even The Cure found themselves in hot water for the dubiously-titled 'Killing An Arab', although they explained it was based on Albert Camus' existentialist novel *The Outsider*. So how did Mark Smith escape the wrath of the moral arbiters? Whether a shock tactic or a succinct stab at the current trend for tokenism, this utterance of the eighties' most taboo word cannot have gone unnoticed. And knowing Mark Smith it was hardly likely to have been a (forgiveable) slip of the tongue. The current climate being what it was, the band inevitably lost a few gigs, and for a small percentage of their audience alienated by such behaviour, this was the proverbial last straw.

"They write in," groaned Smith, "saying, 'I've bought all your records but I've a suspicion you said 'faggot' in an interview, so I don't like you any more'."

Strangely, the expected kangaroo court never materialised, even in the light of recent revelations of how, in pre-Fall days, Smith, Bramah, Baines and Friel used to attend local nightclubs wearing swastika armbands. Judging by the media's previous reactions, this alone deserved an *auto-da-fé*. Instead, the press latched on to this notion of the 'Hip Priest', a tongue-in-cheek title adopted by Smith in the wake of numerous backstage 'confessions' and The Fall's recent surge in popularity.

"In a way," he reflected, "it's a good thing that they've taken to calling me something that I wrote about. Better than for them to call me something of their own invention, which would be much more inferior."

The role of father-confessor was acquired largely by default, an instance where the group's ever-increasing influence seemed to have backfired. Despite their obvious penury, many up-and-coming bands and an enlightened section of the rock establishment now looked up to The Fall. They were survivors, enjoying success on their own

Mark Smith, Nottingham, December 1982

terms, and their ascetic appeal was perfectly in keeping with eighties 'unemployment chic'. Viewed through rose-tinted spectacles, they could have easily been taken for models of independence. But for the big names that squeezed backstage, the important fact was that The Fall never got their hands dirty. Whereas the luminaries had pawned their ideals in exchange for easy cash, The Fall had managed to keep their integrity and their self-respect intact. Smith told *Melody Maker*'s Steve Lake how he discovered that guilt, like the truth, will out.

"I have to hear all the terrible things they've done," he grimaced, "all the little sell-outs. And I'm sitting there with a tight smile saying, 'Oh, don't worry about it, old chap – everybody's got to earn money.' And I'm thinking, 'Get lost!' Y'know, here's us practically starving for the last five years and never compromising an inch and here they are, stinking rich, asking me for pity! Sometimes you really start to despise people . . ."

In the words of 'Hip Priest': 'People only need me when they're down and gone to seed.'

What had always been The Fall's saving grace was that they were innovative, not derivative. Therefore, both press and punters alike were compromised into treating them as artists, which was to say either seriously or else deliver unto them a big fat raspberry. So it was with great eagerness that the music papers picked up on the respect-inducing 'E' which Smith had taken to using lately. The loaded moniker of Mark E. Smith offered greater scope than humble, unassuming Mark Smith, a name already synonymous with, on the one hand, originality and insight, and thorough-going contrariness on the other.

Reporters already seemed hard pushed to convey this balance, so it came as little surprise that musical critique now took a back seat to juicy bombast. Since John Lydon had put on weight and moved into films with *Order Of Death*, Smith was now the only exponent of vehement disgust worth quoting. Everyone else was into issues or hung up on various causes. But Smith didn't entirely relish being type-cast as some kind of boorish Oliver Reed figure, nor did the band like the popular preconceptions held about The Fall as people.

"People do get the impression that The Fall will just attack, verbally or physically, anybody from the establishment," they said with some regret. "We just do it through lyrics, so people steer clear of you."

'Hex Enduction Hour' was, to borrow from 'Hip Priest', 'Bad, unafeared art' – an anthology of rhymes and cadences unique to The Fall, gratifyingly devoid of reference points, American accents and lip-service funk. Smith's appraisal was more modest: "It is packed with typical Fall appreciation of the good things in life, plus the usual niggly, annoying, bitty observations."

As Fall product, it was exactly what we had come to expect, a musical flux rife with vivid images like 'buffalo lips on toast, smiling' (a hamburger) from 'Who Makes The Nazis?'. Yet there was a danger of it all being taken for granted. In articles and even album reviews, songs were lumped together, even glossed over, rather than taken apart. Or perhaps this was one instance where it was nigh on impossible to pitch words against words. Smith had created his own language, but no one was offering the usual translations or interpretations, even though an open invitation – 'Have a bleedin' guess!' – had been scrawled on the album's cover.

Lack of direct criticism starved a potentially larger audience of information, and above all impressions, the common conclusion being a woefully inadequate, 'You either listen to The Fall or you don't.' The Fall were addictive, an escape, possessed of an other-worldliness that demanded explanation, or for the unfamiliar a helpful introduction, not this sink-or-swim attitude.

Describing 'Winter' in the 'Hex' press hand-out as "A tale concerning an insane child who is taken over by a spirit from the mind of a cooped-up alcoholic," Smith offered a background, but no more. So the listener was left to make up his or her own mind about the swelling, bursting tract and the inscrutable passage, 'The mad kid had four lights: the average is two-point-five lights; the mediocre, that's two lights; the sign of genius, that's three lights; there's one light left, that's the science law . . . '

What did it all mean? Why had no one approached close enough to the album to tell of the character assassination of

'Mere Pseud Mag Ed'? Or venture that at 16 minutes 'And This Day' was, in all fairness, unlistenable? Or re-live the barmy tale of 'Jawbone And The Air Rifle' in which a poacher's bad aim defiled the tomb of a religious sect established on the island of Gruinard, where the Ministry of Defence carried out its anthrax experiments . . . Smith rejoiced in the fact there was a whole hour of this impassioned stuff!

By his own admission, every line of every track was crammed with information, but no hack had the wherewithal to wrestle with, 'Who wants to be in a Hovis advert, anyway?' ('Just Step Sideways'), let alone 'Iceland'. Or award top marks for that wonderfully observed line from 'Deer Park' – 'I took a walk down W11; I had to wade through 500 European punks.' It captured the time so perfectly, that awful feeling that imported dye-hairs were looking down their youthful noses.

This tendency to take the overview, as *Sounds*' Dave McCullough pointed out, probably resulted from The Fall being looked upon as a concept. In time, this served to drive an ever greater wedge between the band and Mark E. Smith, or rather the personality cult of Mark E. Smith. Smith was himself painfully aware that he had become the latest victim of this media curse. In addition to 'Hip Priest', he also employed the titles 'Big Personality Face' and 'Mythical Thingy' in an attempt to undermine the inverted icon of Mark E. Smith. "It's a bit of a limitation," Smith revealed to *Sounds*' writer Sandy Robertson. "I can't work in the limelight. It cuts off a lot of my processes: I work better undercover."

What actually tumbled The Fall from the pedestal of 'Hex Enduction Hour' was their follow-up LP, 'Room To Live'. Misconceived and flawed, it was duly panned. Smith, with characteristic perversity, seemed quite pleased. He claimed that its failure to deliver gave the band a much-needed breathing space. All that close scrutiny had become claustrophobic and there were too many hopes pinned on The Fall for their own good. Smith himself felt that the band were on the verge of becoming a supergroup, complete with epic rock sound, a transformation which had recently taken Echo And The Bunnymen out into the wild blue yonder. 'Room To Live' dislodged all those expectations.

Originally, the group planned to bring out a topical 45 'Marquis Cha-Cha'/'Papal Visit', but due to various delays and blunders, only a few thousand copies of this collectors' item were ever pressed. The loose seven-track 'Room To Live' which superseded it, lacked the necessary cohesion to be regarded as an album proper. With a bit of judicious pruning, it could have been a passable EP, but in its unedited form 'Room To Live' sounded like a flabby,

Mark & Brix

overcrowded 12-inch single. The tracks were half-formed and the music ambled along in a well-defined rut of Fallness.

There were, of course, touches of spiteful genius, as in the song 'Solicitor In Studio'. Smith's undiluted vitriol was to be congratulated in the line, 'Young dicks make TV, get them away from me!' which ridiculed those dreadfully earnest youth culture television shows.

'Hard Life In The Country' was a telling premonition of rural violence; 'Straw Dogs' revisited. But 'Marquis Cha-Cha' was undeniably the high point on 'Room To Live'. Its subject matter was the Falklands Conflict. In this story, Mark E. was set up as Marquis Cha-Cha, a latter-day Latin-American Lord Haw-Haw, who broadcast propaganda to H.M. Forces in the South Atlantic. Not surprisingly, the 'loathsome traitor' came to a sticky end: 'So what if I do propaganda? After a few steins I feel better, but that broken-down fan, they never fix it them dumb Latins. There's a bayonet beside my head! There's a guard in the annexe . . . !'

Compared to the indignant but commendable anti-war

outbursts of Crass, to wit the banned 'Sheep Farming In The Falklands' and 'How Does It Feel (To Be The Mother Of The 1000 Dead)?', 'Marquis Cha-Cha' reacted to the situation with wit and intelligence. Like Robert Wyatt's sensitive rendition of the Elvis Costello song 'Shipbuilding', it kept a respectful distance, handling the war and its victims with compassion. The irony was that just a few months before, in the song 'Jawbone And The Air-Rifle', the rabbit-killer had said, 'There's been no war for 40 years . . . '

Regarding his lyric writing, Smith maintained that he still wrote in the same manner, "cutting up newspapers and stuf', but confessed that before their 1981 American tour he had suffered from a crisis of confidence.

"After America," he told *NME*'s Barney Hoskyns, "I stopped taking writing so seriously. I was taking myself too seriously, especially in America. We played universities and these guys go, 'You're one of the best writers I've read in my fucking life.' And nobody's ever said that to me here, nobody ever gives me a compliment. But after they say that to you in America, you stop worrying about it, you know . . . " Smith's writing was haphazard, inspired, but above all prolific. He often wrote "great dense chunks of prose", sometimes editing these mammoth texts down to manageable lyric size.

In addition to copious amounts of reading matter Smith devoured, he cited among his influences all abuses of the English language, "like the letters page in the *Daily Mirror* and those cheap cash and carry signs with inverted commas where you don't need them." If it was at all incongruous, it would fit nicely into a Fall song.

A year after their trip to the States, The Fall took flight from the UK once again. This time they undertook a seven-week tour of Australia and New Zealand during the summer, playing 26 gigs in all. The Fall had a certain following in Australia, but Mark E. Smith had definite misgivings about their reception.

"The country was like a perverted Britain," he told *NME*'s Richard Cook. "The Aussies were expecting a British new wave type band and they didn't get on with what we were doing at all. I think we actually had more fans before we went than after we came back."

Australia also had plenty of home-grown talent and a fiercely loyal following even among record company moguls. The only accepted outsiders were the really big names from the northern hemisphere, so there wasn't an awful lot of scope for an 'alternative' band like The Fall. Even leather rockers The Stranglers had been hounded out of Queensland, Australia's answer to the Deep South. Still, it was comforting to know that punk's shock waves had not completely dissipated yet.

PAINTWORK **WORDS OF EXPECTATION**

Hammersmith Palais, November 1985

Smith used to be pally with antipodean expatriate Nick Cave of The Birthday Party, but let the acquaintance slip when Cave started hanging out with Soft Cell. "But Australians, y'know," said Smith, understandingly, "they have no morals." The Fall, as it turned out, got on much better with New Zealand.

"Everything's so slow there," beamed Smith, "it's like 1954. We were in the fucking Top 20 there, which means about 600 records sold, but it's a big thing. It was full of surprises. I mean, there's loads of skinheads there."

To commemorate the visit, their Auckland gig was taped and later produced as the album 'In A Hole' on Flying Nun records. However, it was perhaps most notable for the photograph on its cover. It showed a jaunty Marc Riley, bag in hand, stepping out across some airport lounge. After six years with the band, he'd been given his marching orders.

"His leaving was a conscious move," clarified Smith. "I knew what I was doing."

"He's got to have everything his own way," countered Riley in an interview with *Jamming*'s Dave Jennings. "If ever you stand up to him, you may get away with it at the time, but he'll take it out on you in another way."

Apparently, Lieutenant Riley and Captain Smith had not seen eye to eye for some time, particularly in regard to the group's musical direction. Increasing friction had led to an altercation in a disco on the Australian leg of their tour. 'Dare to dance on an Aussie dance floor,' was how Riley alluded to the event in the pointedly-titled 'Jumper Clown', one of the songs he performed with his new band The Creepers. At the time of his departure, many wits had given Riley the nickname Lucifer, the inference being that he had fallen from God's right hand. But for the time being The Creepers weren't bound for obscurity.

Despite sustained hostility from Mark E. Smith, Marc Riley conceded to *Melody Maker*'s Frank Worrall that, "The best thing The Fall had was the power. That's what I aim to get. To get people coming to me."

Sounds' correspondent Jack Barron discovered that Smith wasn't always damning about his former colleague: music remained the primary consideration.

"Marc was great," mused Smith, "but I felt really restricted by the tune patterns and the pop song idiom which he was injecting into the group. Once you start revolving around the axis of a tune, the rest of your stuff is fucked."

This certainly seemed true of 'Joker Hysterical Face' off 'Room To Live'. Ordinarily, the two parties seemed content to snipe at each other, pride and basic stubbornness precluding any chance of them agreeing to disagree. Smith in particular never let up. "It was a lot easier on the ears when he went," was a typical comment. "And you just didn't see this big flappy mong walking around the stage any more, distracting everybody's attention. Saved a lot of money on equipment as well."

Riley's involvement with 'Hex' was probably the main reason why Smith was given to slagging it off barely 12 months after he'd been singing its praises. And for years The Fall encored with the ultimate (and possibly libellous) put-down, 'Hey! Marc Riley!'

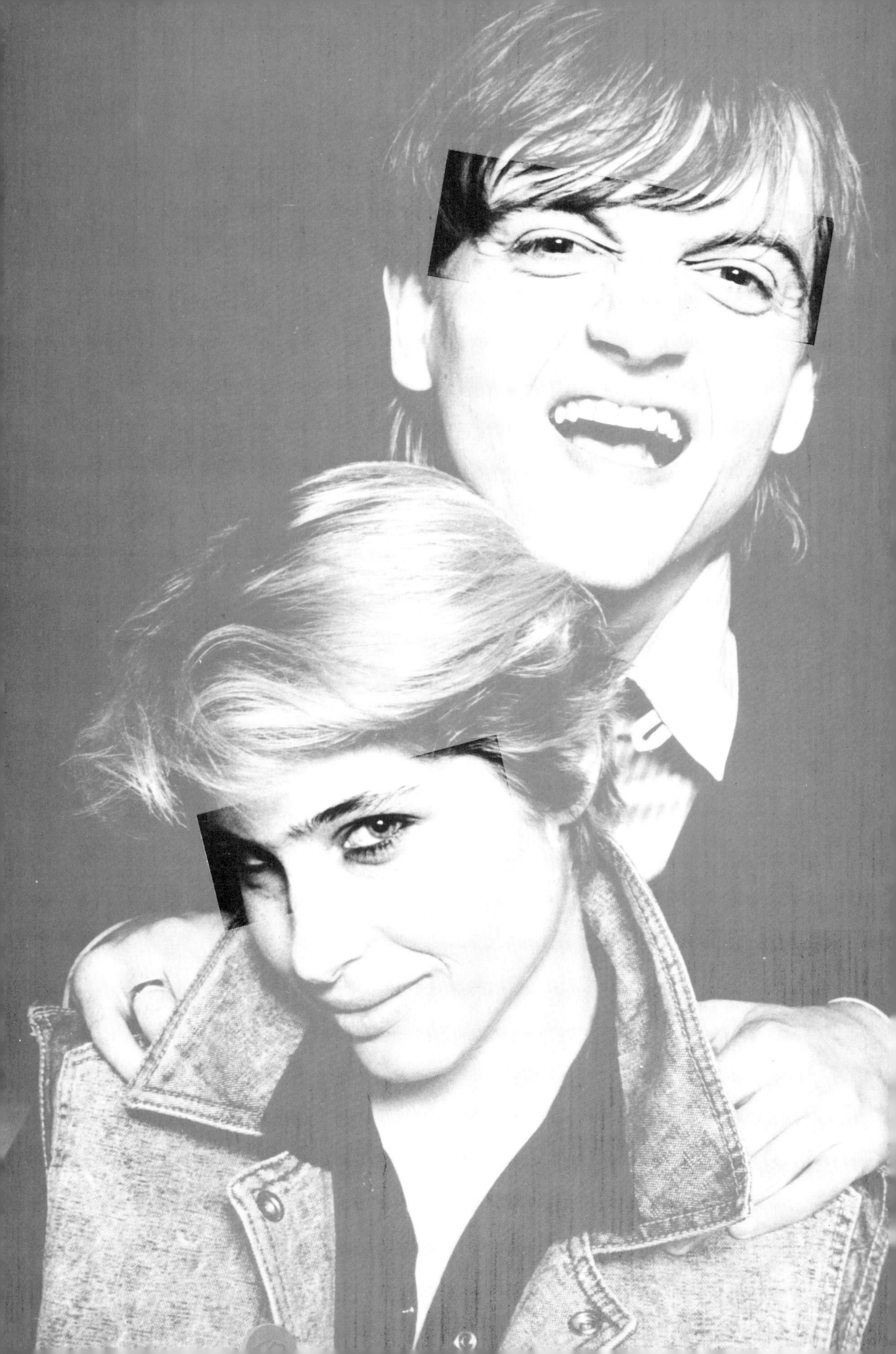

'And the Dutch are weeping in four languages at least!' –
'Tempo House'.

CHAPTER 6
GODZONE

"Now Marc's left it's a new project," Mark Smith declared to *Melody Maker*'s Frank Worrall. "There was too much melody. Now I'm going to erase it and get down to a very biased one channel of noise which I've been after for years."

The Fall didn't really surface again until the winter of 1982. During the intervening period interest in the band waned and they could afford to reorientate their music, secure in the knowledge that their devoted following wasn't about to desert them.

NME's Richard Cook found Smith at the helm, firmly pushing the band towards the ultimate Fall sound. "It usually makes sense, what he says," offered Karl Burns. "If it doesn't, you pretend it does and he doesn't notice."

"I put a lot of pressure on them," admitted Smith. "I don't get argumentative, but I do it so everyone's wound up. For example, you hear LPs by groups who've fought all the way through and they're the weakest things in the world. All that's going to happen is the producer and the engineer step in." The band's foundations had set hard long since, with stalwarts Karl Burns and the Brothers Hanley rocksteady in their duties. Craig Scanlon scraped his guitar fluently across the wider spaces and rhythmic openings. Smith may have been playing the perfectionist, but he was aware of the talent at his disposal.

"The most original aspect of The Fall," he ventured, "is Steve on the bass. I've never heard a bass player like him in my life. I don't have to tell him what to play, he just knows. He is The Fall sound."

Since Riley had set up shop elsewhere, Smith had adopted a more paternal attitude towards the rest of the band, whom he liked to call 'the lads'. But this didn't lessen the admiration he held for his musicians: "They can translate what I want into something even better."

Even without this almost complete control Smith had always dominated in interviews as well as on-stage. *NME*'s Richard Cook put the question to him: "Why is it that The Fall is so completely Smith's vehicle – why does the rest of the group seem so anonymous?"

"You've met musicians, for God's sake!" interjected manager Kay Carroll. "It's like, Craig plays guitar really well, and Mark plays his brain really well."

"I'm not sure why it is," added Smith, thoughtfully. "It surprises me. It's not as if they don't try and be personalities."

Mr & Mrs Smith, September 1983

Early interviews had, in keeping with the democratic vogue of the day, featured all band members. But as Smith became the natural spokesman for the band he found it increasingly awkward to hold forth in front of his companions. Yet as Edwin Pouncey of *Sounds* learned, Smith wasn't the 'print-head' one might have expected.

"I don't read my own interviews," he confessed. "I get the band to read them and tell me what they were like and what they think of them. I get a bit embarrassed. They make jokes, which I think is very healthy. Craig always says things to me like, 'You're sure you didn't want to talk about yourself a bit more?'"

It had quickly become second nature for them to defer and they now felt patronised whenever a journalist was wont to toss a question in their direction. Interviews with other members of The Fall had been arranged in the past, as Mark Smith told *Sounds*' Jack Barron, though the exercise with a former associate of Barron's had not gone at all according to plan.

"This reporter," chuckled Smith, "was obsessed with getting an interview with the rest of the band. So I set it all up. But when she came to do the interview, two of the band had forgotten about it and driven home and the others had all gone off for the day. She ended up interviewing Karl and the driver. All she got was three hours of Karl calling the driver a fucking Jew, grabbing the guy in a neck hold and just being really horrible."

'Wings', September 1983

Mark Smith, Manchester, September 1983

The biggest obstacle to surmount when tackling The Fall was that they had long-established routines, clearly-defined stations and they weren't about to betray the enigma now. Above all, they had an utter conviction in, and love of, the music they were producing. Interviews were an occupational hazard and part of pop music's fickle, fashionable side, of which The Fall were the antithesis. The Fall's existence was as fragile as that of any band, but it had now become a way of life for them, as spiritually rewarding and wildly frustrating as any worthwhile job ought to have been. This came across in every new piece of music, a balance between apparent effortlessness and stern concentration, a marriage won through the gifts of improvisation and hard work. Nothing stood in the way of The Fall.

"They're like me," said Smith, proudly. "They're big Fall fans. I'm a big Fall fan – it sounds ridiculous, I know. It's a weird thing, it's hard to explain. It's like the group is now really good because none of them are in it for the money (ha!) or the fame. They're all in it because they want to be in The Fall, which sounds a simple thing but which is a great thing!"

The Fall had no doubts that they were fit enough for sporadic touring on the Continent. The band played in Switzerland, Belgium, and Holland, where they had always been especially popular. However, gigs arranged in Germany, which the band acknowledged as their true 'second market', were cancelled due to their fans' boisterousness on previous visits.

In mid-1983, the group renewed their acquaintance with the record-buying public with a single entitled 'The Man Whose Head Expanded'. It was their first record since the badly-received 'Room To Live', which had been released on Kamera Records. The label had since slid into bankruptcy and the band, after a bit of cajoling, were now back with Rough Trade. The single's B-side, 'Ludd Gang', featured Hanley's distorted bass, its notes riveted into the superstructure of the song. This use of distortion, a treatment also favoured by New Order's Peter Hook, was a mark of The Fall tentatively widening their musical vocabulary.

They weren't known for experimentation and Smith had fought shy of the ubiquitous synthesizers and increasingly popular digital sequencers for years. The band were neither technophobes nor acoustic purists: they merely wished to have control over their instruments rather than employ technology for its own sake. Machines only encouraged human beings' natural inclination to laziness. And the music produced by such machines was cursed with rigidity and bland uniformity. Sadly, universal acceptance was its birthright.

Within The Fall, new technology was kept to a minimum, featuring on 'The Man Whose Head Expanded' only as irritating punctuation, as it had done on the introduction to 'Fortress' on 'Hex'. The tinny, micro-chip percussion made a mockery of pub culture entertainments, video games in particular: 'Turn that bloody blimey Space Invader off!' implored the frazzled character in the song. *Sounds'* Jack Barron had Mark Smith throw some light on this fevered song.

"It's about this fella," he explained, "who's been fucked up by too much misinformation posing as real information. And then it goes into this obvious paranoia trip where he thinks this bloke from a soap opera is ripping off his lines. But his thoughts are too intense for him to do anything about it. That's why the vocals are very untogether.

"I'm a bit pissed off that people find the song indecipherable," he added. "I find it pretty clear."

Like so many other Fall songs, 'The Man Whose Head Expanded' contained a humorous gem. It was good to see that Mark E. Smith was amused by his own material: it made him seem human and somehow fallible. Never trust people who can't laugh at their own jokes. "I enjoy the line about the 'sociological memory man'," grinned Smith. "Did you ever hear those sports memory men who used to stand up and people would shout at them, 'Who won the World Cup in 1920?' Now, like, you get sociological guys telling you about how many people didn't have houses in 1945!"

The follow-up, 'Kicker Conspiracy', a double single

PAINTWORK **GODZONE**

Mark & Brix, October 1985

PAGE **63**

PAINTWORK **GODZONE**

housed in a gatefold sleeve, appeared within a few months. In an attempt to appease fans' perennial requests for the Peel session version of 'Container Drivers', recorded at the tail end of 1980, the BBC were persuaded to allow Rough Trade to press it. It appeared as the retrospective half of the package, together with 'New Puritan', the song that had sparked off revelations about 'grotesque peasants' and ended with, 'The villagers dance round pre-fabs and laugh through twisted mouths' on 'Jawbone And The Air Rifle'.

The topical 'Kicker Conspiracy' peeled away football's mask of respectability and stated that bad administration was to blame for its lousy public image, not violence on the terraces.

"I don't agree with this idea that football is something for all the family to enjoy," said Smith. "If you want a hot dog and all your family with you then you go to the park, not a football match."

A Manchester City supporter in his youth, Smith could hold forth on the national game just as passionately as he did on the music business. As *Melody Maker*'s Barry McIlheney once commented, Smith was always "ready to cast a suitably jaundiced eye over everything and everyone from the Second World War to Terry Venables."

A video for 'Kicker Conspiracy' appeared on The Fall's 'Perverted By Language Bis' compilation. Filmed at lowly Burnley Football Club's Turf Moor ground (Old Trafford would have been far too glamorous a setting), it opened with an hilarious shot of the trainer's bench. As Smith performed for the camera, Paul Hanley hunched forward chewing gum, playing the part of concerned coach to satirical perfection. The video also featured emotive shots of barbed wire and the crowd-restraining spikes surmounting the terrace enclosures.

From Mark E. Smith's point of view the Football Association and the Government's "hysterical reaction to this natural pastime" solved very little. (As Marquis Cha-Cha had said of Argentina, 'Football and beer much superior.') In lieu of fielding decent teams, they were naïve enough to rely on British fans abroad acting as ambassadors for our great sporting nation (cue stock footage of cheering post-War crowds). The hooligans were merely scapegoats for management that to Smith's mind, "mercilessly gunned down any talent." He had a great sympathy for mavericks like George Best, who was eventually hounded out of football because of his disreputable behaviour. Smith once met the former Manchester United star at a club. "He said to me that if he pulled 40,000 people a week he should be able to do what he wanted and he was right."

Smith's other hero was Tony Coleman . . . "the wild

Mark Smith, Manchester, September 1983

PAINTWORK **GODZONE**

Mark · E & Brix · E Smith, September 1983

man of City, the Keith Moon of soccer – completely ungovernable. He used to vomit before every game because he was that nervous."

'Kicker Conspiracy' was complemented perfectly by 'Wings', modestly vaunted by the band as their best recording to date. Dominated by the swarf from Scanlon's guitar, 'Wings' was a gripping Fall fantasy. The 'flabby wings' in question enabled the user to alter the time-space continuum, only with overuse the wings eventually lost their power and became thereafter a burden. A cautionary tale indeed.

Besides displaying Smith's new-found love of history, 'Wings' showed him to be the most daring lyricist around. The tradition that Mark E. Smith adhered to was firmly rooted in the expansive field of literature, not rock's pained and puerile analyses of boy-girl relationships. But was his recent marriage to Brix about to change all this?

During their 1983 summer tour of America, The Fall lost a manager and Mark E. Smith gained a wife. Kay Carroll's decision to remain in Boston shocked the group, while reports that one of rock's most unconventional figures had actually jumped the broomstick had a similar effect on the rockbiz literati. Until it finally sunk in with Brix being showcased on The Fall's late 1983 UK tour, the question, 'Is that blonde girl really Mark E. Smith's wife?' continued to expose our reactionary attitude towards the institution of marriage.

People tended to look upon their favourite groups as immutable objects, immortal super-beings. Small wonder, then, that the majority were forever disappointed. Fans, many of whom never wanted one note of their cherished music to alter, believed that change was essentially bad for bands, that it might wreck their supposedly fragile creative processes. And they had the gall to complain whenever something new came along, be it a musical influence or love, preferring nostalgia to learning afresh. Basically, all people had ever wanted was to have their brains set in aspic.

The couple met in a Chicago bar when Brix stumbled upon Mark E. getting blitzed after what he thought was a poor Fall performance. Brix related her first impressions to *Melody Maker* scribe Steve Lake.

"Mark just looked completely dishevelled," she remembered, fondly. "He had a bottle of beer in both hands and he was sort of staggering around in crumpled up clothes. And I said to myself, 'God, if he's not a junkie, I don't know who is!' But it didn't put me off somehow.

"I don't know, I don't usually talk to strange men in bars. It was just . . . fate. Well, we went to a party afterwards and just argued. Disagreed about everything. We were completely different people, from completely different backgrounds. We didn't think we had anything in common."

On examining her background, this certainly appears to be true: Brix came from a wealthy Californian family, which had broken up when she was young; she was once a model for an upmarket LA fashion store and in her spare time she developed her latent talent for buying clothes. In marked contrast to her husband, Brix took pride in her glamorous appearance. However, a strong bond had been formed and they married without further ado. It only remained for Brix to disband her erstwhile group Burden Of Proof and emigrate to pluvial Manchester.

The speed with which the diminutive Brix joined The Fall was doubly disarming: there was, after all, a bad tradition of wives in bands. Just ask The Beatles. Naturally, there were those who cried nepotism, but the opposite was in fact true. Smith had demurred on having his new wife in the group, but the other band members were all for it. As he told *Record Mirror*'s Andy Strickland, "It was strange, really, because even Karl seemed keen on Brix and he's never got a good word to say about anyone."

Brix, too, was acutely aware that joining The Fall would be like jumping on to a moving object and keeping her balance. She confided her misgivings to *Melody Maker*'s Steve Lake.

"I felt that I would ruin it!" recalled Brix. "How could I, an American girl, come into something that was so well defined, so special and so pure? I was really afraid. I felt I didn't have enough technical skill for one thing. But it turned out to be so easy, like dropping the last piece into a jigsaw puzzle."

With Brix accepted into the band as a second guitarist, The Fall were set to undergo the biggest change in their seven-year history. The only murmurings of discontent came from the die-hard pro-Riley lobby, soon to become an extinct breed. Smith remained unmoved, determined. "The Fall have always changed," he told *NME*'s Mat Snow, "and there's people who can never bleedin' handle it. It's the story of The Fall."

Punters didn't have to wait long to make up their minds about the brave new Fall. Those who hadn't caught up with the band on their latest tour, and who hadn't joined in the fun of 'What's a computer? – Eat yourself fitter!', found Brix's influence on The Fall's latest LP 'Perverted By Language'. The name Brix E-for-Elise Smith appeared on the credits of 'Hotel Bloedel', a song she had co-written during the band's last visit to southern Germany after spending an unforgettable night in a Nuremburg hotel.

Mark E. Smith remembered how their room had been filled with "this choking smell – you'd have sworn there'd been a murder there." Brix agreed. "And at six in the morning there were these ghastly screams. I was sure the place was haunted. Mark lit cigarettes and put them all around the room to fight off the horrible smell. When it got light we looked out of the window and saw an old woman coming across the courtyard carrying a sack of blood into the hotel . . ."

It transpired they had checked in next door to an abattoir. This was the stuff great Fall songs were made of, half-truths, fear and good old-fashioned mystery. 'Hotel Bloedel' had the same malevolent air as their 1977 number 'Various Times', a moral little tune which featured a man who became a concentration camp guard to avoid the war. Hence it was doubly ironic that while on tour The Fall's bus broke down in the town of Dachau, leaving them stranded there for a week.

If ever there was a title that summed up The Fall it was 'Perverted By Language'. And if there was one song that encapsulated The Fall's spirit it was 'Hexen Definitive', here laid to rest on the album's second side. It really belonged to a bygone era, but its vituperative power was undiminished: 'You're all clutching at straws, you won't drive me insane; you know nothing about it, it's not your domain; don't confuse yourself with someone who's got something to say.'

Stylistically, Mark E. Smith's lyrics were in a class of their own. He was, as Gavin Martin of *NME* stated, "A writer with a rapper's quick-witted spontaneity, a rapper with a writer's breadth and alacrity."

Plenty of Smith's contemporaries, notably Talking Heads' David Byrne and Morrissey of The Smiths, were undoubtedly gifted songwriters, evoking some of rock's most eloquent and subtle imagery, but their adherence to the pseudo-poetic conventions of songwriting meant they often didn't match up to Smith's articulate originality. Though Scritti Politti's Green came up with some inspired semantic twists, like 'his hammer and his popsicle', his approach to lyric writing was plainly academic – who else would have written a song entitled 'Hegemony' or a number about an obscure French semanticist ('Jacques Derrida')? Elizabeth Fraser of The Cocteau Twins enjoyed similar playful word games, but use of her beautiful uncontrollable voice as an instrument left the listener veiled in an atmosphere of aesthetics and insubstantial images.

However, it would be incorrect to assume that Smith's songwriting was unselfconscious. Far from it. He frequently employed the so-called cut-up technique, as did avant-garde funksters 23 Skidoo, which had been practised for decades by influential writer William Burroughs in his more bizarre novels like *The Soft Machine*. Smith, too, dismantled syntax at every turn and re-edited sentences to suit his own dissembling purposes. Yet it was Smith's snarling delivery, the gut feeling that came across in nearly every Fall song, that ultimately lent credence to his bilious, fragmented outpourings. Brix, who hadn't let 'Slates' leave her turntable for a fortnight when she first played it, put it more bluntly: "I think he shines like a star in a world of muck".

"Any of our lines is worth 10 of anybody else's," added Smith. "There's 10 times more words in there!"

On 'Perverted By Language' Mark Smith once again proved he was master of his craft. An ability to use words as blunt instruments, as opposed to painterly devices or catch-phrases, conveyed the raw talent of a genuine expressionist. A clear connection could be seen between his writing and the bold, uncomfortable paintings of young artist Claus Castenskiold, whose works began to appear on Fall record covers.

Without examining his navel, always the biggest danger

of introversion, Smith put over an intensely personal perspective of the world, a legacy of images that were disturbingly familiar. The cathartic scene depicted in 'Smile', for instance, was recognisable to anyone who had experienced fear within a night club's matt black walls. 'Take the chicken run!' goaded Smith. 'Take the chicken run to the toilet . . . !' The music calmed, nerves tightened, pulses raced – 'Sparks off, repeal gun laws in my brain; sparks off, give us a gun if I got one. Damn! Grin . . . '

"Like, we went to New York," elaborated Smith. "And I know it's violent, but it was fucking safer than Manchester or anywhere in Yorkshire has ever been at half 11. When the pubs shut it's fucking deadly!"

Their video 'Perverted By Language Bis', was the perfect accompaniment to the album and tempered all the intellectualising that appeared in the music press. More than anything else their video dispelled any notion that The Fall were a bunch of pop-stars, picturing the band in their natural habitat (pub/club/pool table/living room).

Surprisingly, video captured the Fall ethos better than any other medium. Their attempts at genre pop video were more like home movies: 'Wings' was shot in a pub, and while the band were being served at the bar, Smith slouched against the flock wallpaper in the snug, miming.

'Eat Y'Self Fitter' was equally unprofessional, and 10 times as disgusting, with Karl Burns salivating copiously in close-up and the make-up department running to boils on Craig Scanlon's face. To their credit, they sustained this revolting spectacle for the full six-and-a-half minutes of the song, without the aid of special effects or pretentious art direction. The absence of shame echoed Smith's proud boast – 'We are The Fall!' – on the album track 'Neighbourhood Of Infinity'.

"I worry about pride and dignity," said Smith. "I don't like it that people who are obviously decent are having to go into selling computers when they would formerly have gone into a trade." 'Perverted By Language Bis' was comprised mainly of live footage, the highlight of which was a rambling 'Tempo House' shot at Factory Records' Hacienda club in Manchester. The same live version of this song appeared on the album, a song which saw The Fall again exploring new musical fields, testing the ground beyond the safe boundaries of rock.

"When you invent your own music and do your own arrangements," ventured Smith, "you start to approach a kind of 'classical' form. It's always been ideal. The second side of 'Perverted' is getting close, y'know. The balance of tonal and atonal stuff, melodic fragments and free-form bits, complex texts and simple music, and vice versa . . . "

The video compilation was pieced together under the auspices of Factory offshoot Ikon Video, whose previous

Mark & Brix

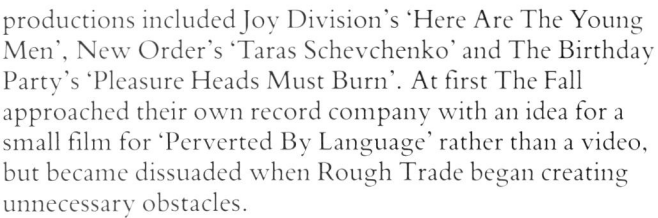

productions included Joy Division's 'Here Are The Young Men', New Order's 'Taras Schevchenko' and The Birthday Party's 'Pleasure Heads Must Burn'. At first The Fall approached their own record company with an idea for a small film for 'Perverted By Language' rather than a video, but became dissuaded when Rough Trade began creating unnecessary obstacles.

"This was the time when Rough Trade were trying to be Pop Label Number One," recalled Smith. "They were going, 'Aztec Camera's video cost £7,000', and we were saying that we didn't mean like that. Then they said, 'Well, you've got to have a union crew.' Why have you got to have a union crew, y'know?"

In desperation they turned to Ikon cameraman Malcolm Whitehead and his associate Claude Bessy, who ended up funding the project themselves. The nominal £500 Rough Trade had sent them away with was spent solely on props. As a promotional exercise Mark E. Smith didn't think it would be that successful: he was in any case more interested in experimentation.

"Have you seen the Open University programmes?" he enthused, to *Sounds*' Edwin Pouncey. "They have a graph on the screen for about five minutes. I think that's fantastic. I thought it would be great to have something like that and just the music playing. Not flashing or anything, just a graph."

Rough Trade's unhelpfulness and general lack of enthusiasm eventually resulted in the band walking out on their deal early in 1984. By that time, Smith was so demoralised he had ceased writing. The Fall were broke, support seemed to be waning and they were in half a mind to call it a day. Matters came to a head shortly after 'Perverted By Language' saw release in November 1983, when the band wised up to Rough Trade having broken most of the promises made when The Fall had been invited back into the stable.

They had been encouraged to return to the label with assertions that this time around Rough Trade would lay on the best recording facilities, even get them on television, claiming that they would do all they could to help The Fall break out of their restrictive cult mould. "We thought, 'Oh well, this sounds interesting, they're thinking about us at least.' So we go back to them and after four weeks it's the same old story, except worse this time because they were concentrating on that one big act (The Smiths). They'd gotten the idea that they wanted to be pop makers, which left us in a bit of a mess. All the bands on the label at that time will tell you the same story. So I said no more – I'd rather retire than work with them again."

The first priority of the New Year then became to find a new record label, though the longer they delayed getting signed up, the more distasteful the idea became. "You start putting your energy into courting bloody cretins," griped Smith. "The Fall have never kissed arse, or ingratiated themselves. We've paid for it, but I don't feel bad about it."

However, without a record company's financial backing The Fall simply couldn't survive. During this period only gigging kept their heads above water. To their delight a hastily arranged UK tour was a virtual sell-out. Curiosity, it seemed, still drew many to the band, and in Brix there was an added novelty value. "That's always been our main strength," reflected Smith, "people coming along to have a look. Thank God there are a lot of nosy people around!"

Having had enough of the independent scene, The Fall were now on the lookout for a sympathetic major company with decent resources. Initially, they found themselves looking towards America.

"I think there are a lot of good big labels," expounded Smith to *NME*'s Graham Lock. "The American labels impress me. At least they're honest about what they do. In Britain the whole structure is Victorian. The idea of sending a band out on a tour that costs half a million pounds in order to make three-quarters of a million is just a waste of energy. The Americans tend to just hype somebody, make a million, then piss off."

In a typically perverse turn of events, it appeared that the great British institution of The Fall would be signing to premier Soul label Motown. There were even rumours of a £46,000 advance. But it came to nothing. After some consideration, Smith told *Melody Maker*'s Colin Irwin that the man behind the big desk over in Detroit had turned them down with a back-handed compliment: "I see no commercial potential in this band whatsoever."

"The funny thing was," chuckled Smith, "this guy at Motown asked for some of our old stuff to listen to and the only thing I had was 'Hex Enduction Hour'. Practically the first line on that is, 'Where are the obligatory niggers?' – I thought, 'When they hear that, we've had it!'"

Fortunately for The Fall Beggars Banquet came up with the proverbial offer they couldn't refuse and they've been with them ever since. By the end of May 1984 the band were out on vinyl again with the single 'Oh! Brother', a revamped, some said overly commercial, version of a song they used to play in their earlier days. 'God-Box', on the B-side, was one of Brix's old songs, for which Mark E. Smith promptly wrote a fresh set of lyrics about religion on television.

"American TV," said Smith, "you have it on all the time. I could watch those religious programmes forever, they're fantastic. What I found though was that every time I put

Mark & Brix

Advertisement for PERVERTED BY LANGUAGE

one on, no matter how much I wanted to watch and laugh at it, I'd fall asleep. I thought it must be something to do with staying up late, but when we got back to England they had a documentary on about these American religious programmes at half past eight and I fell asleep again with my tea in front of me. That's the appeal of these shows, that's why they're successful – they comfort people."

The contract with Beggars Banquet had, however, been 'won' with 'C.R.E.E.P.', which for some unexplained reason sold remarkably well. This catchy number appeared shortly after 'Oh! Brother', and when bracketed with that single it occurred to many that The Fall were about to enter a commercial phase. The band, of course, denied they were after a hit, saying that it was purely coincidence that their first two releases on Beggars Banquet were more pop-orientated than recent offerings.

"The aim of 'C.R.E.E.P.' wasn't to get into the Top 30," stressed Smith. "The idea was to get a bleedin' contract with a song I particularly liked!"

The Fall, it seemed, had at last landed on their feet. The leaden air with which the band began 1984 had all but evaporated and they were now progressing more confidently than ever. After the upsets of the previous 12 months The Fall were now settling down to a period of relative stability. Consequently, their creative output mushroomed, with Brix's musical and lyrical contributions adding an extra dimension to their ever-changing sound. Mark E. Smith was in no doubt that Brix was responsible for the band being back on course again, united and unfearing. Her worth at this time could not be over-estimated.

"Strange," mused Smith, "with the group I'm a lot more understanding, I don't try to control every move they make. I haven't got time any more because I'm married. It's done me a lot of good though. I'd have been fucking dead by now, dead as a post."

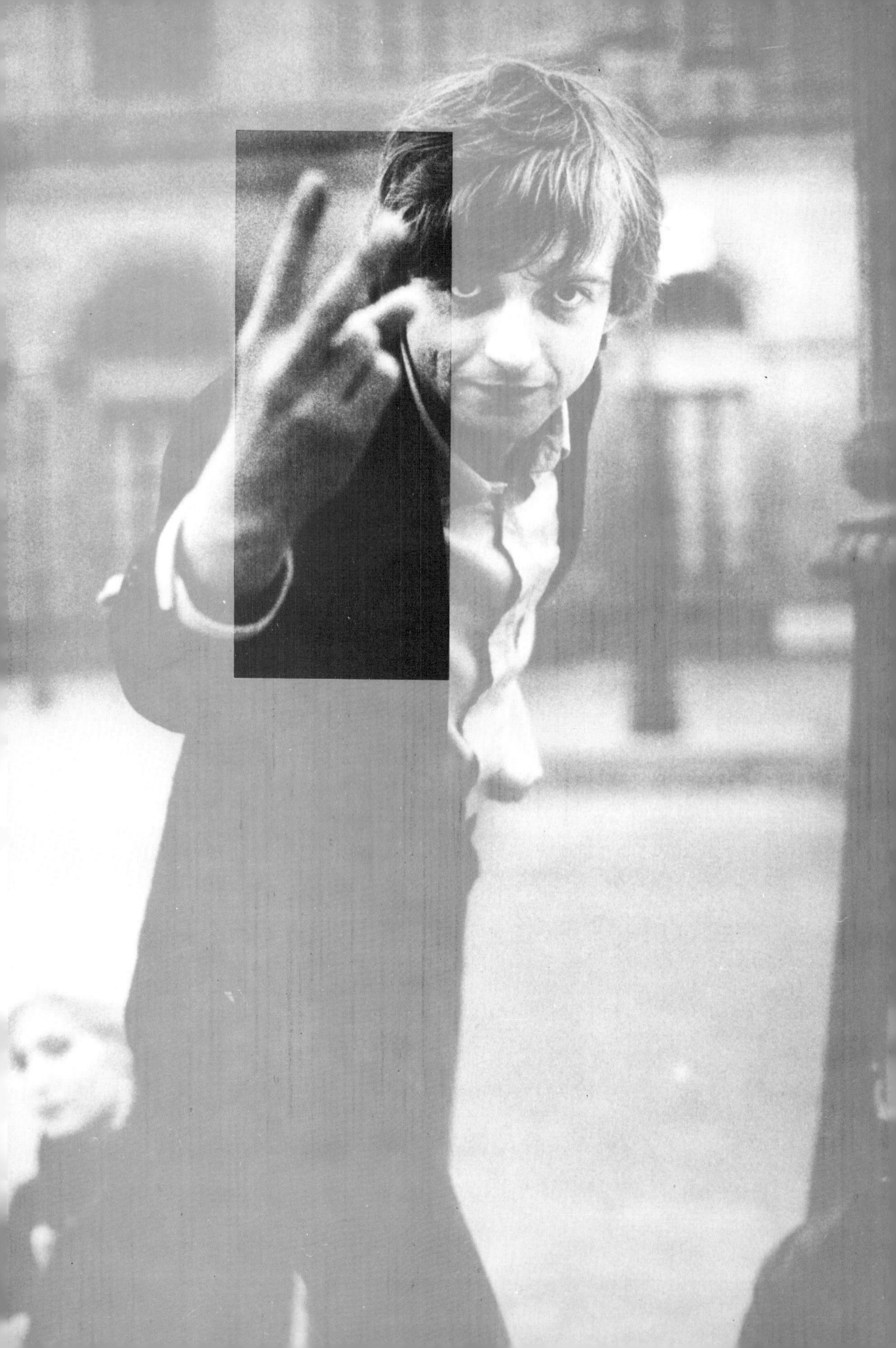

'Welcome to the US 80's – 90's.' – 'US 80's – 90's'.

CHAPTER 7
THE PAY-OFF

The success of 'C.R.E.E.P.' proved to be both a turning point and a talking point. Written at the time of 'Perverted By Language', Smith had been saving it for a rainy day, a time when The Fall might need to reassert their presence. As it happened, 'C.R.E.E.P.' jumped straight out of the radio and up the charts, albeit the fag end. The net result was that it got their name bandied about, particularly among a younger audience, and doubled their record sales. However, when the single was reviewed on Radio One's *Roundtable*, presenter Richard Skinner inadvertently plunged the group into boiling water by announcing that 'C.R.E.E.P.' was about The Smiths.

"Where'd you get this from?" demanded Smith down the phone. "You bloody say a retraction!" Which he did. Relations between members of the Mancunian Holy Trinity – The Fall, The Smiths and New Order – were strained enough without this kind of helpful remark. Earlier associations (Smith first got to know Morrissey when he was plain Steven) had since been replaced by a respectful distance.

"I used to hang around with the drummer out of New Order," Smith told *Record Mirror*'s Nancy Culp, "and we used to have a great time. But it was, like, closed off. It was like getting to know a Russian Communist leader. When I went to talk to him there'd be three roadies in front of him trying to get me out of the way! It was like a school yard!"

On 'C.R.E.E.P.', producer John Leckie endowed The Fall with a new, polished sound. Under his guidance both band and label were able to realise their recognised potential. For Beggars Banquet bringing out The Fall's hidden articulacy was perhaps their prime consideration. Speaking to *Sounds*' reporter Edwin Pouncey, Mark E. Smith explained that this appreciation had been well received within the band. "We went down there thinking they wouldn't be all that interested," he recalled. "But they were. What they saw, which was good, was that the sound was there, it just needed to come. That's what I liked about 'Oh! Brother' – it was the first time Karl's drums sounded like you were in the same room as him."

This was in marked contrast to their last venture with Rough Trade. 'Perverted By Language' had been dogged by technical problems all through production. After the event the band complained bitterly about having been booked into a sub-standard studio . . . "The machinery was that fucked that on 'Strife Knot' you can actually hear the

Mark Smith, September 1985

Mark & Brix, October 1984

previous take underneath." 'Eat Y'Self Fitter' had run to seven takes because of the tape heads sticking during recording. With Beggars Banquet the group seemed to be getting a better deal all round.

In addition, The Fall found a new outlet for 'Perverted By Language', along with 'Hex Enduction Hour' and 'Room To Live' (originally released on the now-defunct Kamera label), through Line Records of Hamburg. The group had had dealings with Line, who specialised in 1960's US West Coast obscurities, over the past three years. Impressed with their enthusiasm and competence The Fall opted to use their services rather than trust to a better-connected organisation like Rough Trade Deutschland, because, "Rough Trade Deutschland are the same as Rough Trade England: a pack of dicks, basically."

On the home front, Smith took over the role of manager, which he found both stimulating and a diversion from pre-gig worries about the music. In confessing that keeping The Fall going, both logistically and financially, became at times almost an obsession with him, Smith again stated that the world outside the band held little allure for him. For example, he placed politics on an even lower footing than the music business. He voted Conservative at the last election because the local Labour Party candidate's antics had incensed him so much.

"I used to call him Jesus Christ In Reverse," explained Smith, "because some fascist pinned him up. He had marks on his hands which he used to show everybody. And at Labour meetings he used to stand up, take out this rotting fish and say, 'What about the Grimsby fishermen?' A complete charlatan."

He also changed his attitude to live performances, literally forcing himself to face the audience, having come to the conclusion that sheer concentration might easily be mistaken for rudeness.

"Being on stage shouldn't be a pleasure," Smith told *NME*'s Gavin Martin. "It should be your craft. I don't consider it performing at all, performers are like other people to me. It's the same with writing, too. There should always be a fear involved in what you're doing, a fear that maybe you shouldn't be there at all."

Facing the audience was, however, one of the few concessions the band were prepared to make. Although Smith on occasion dropped his trusty pullover in favour of a pink lurex shirt, and Brix's peroxided hair gave The Fall a more fashionable look, they still refused to bound around on stage or employ anything but the most spartan lighting. But as *Melody Maker*'s Steve Lake rightly pointed out, "The sight of musicians playing demanding music is quite visual enough." Encouragingly, the absence of pompous spectacle didn't deter the newer, younger converts from making the traditional post-concert pilgrimage back-stage.

Mark E. Smith registered his bemusement at the group's shift in appeal with *NME*'s Richard Cook. "Yesterday we were getting mithered by all these little kids," he said, "all about seven or eight. They were saying, 'Why didn't you do 'Pat-Trip Dispenser'?' and stuff. Wanted autographs, too. So I said to Craig, 'Get those little kids away from me! It's bloody perverse.' And he said, 'They all know our names, y'know.' That's what *Smash Hits* does for you. I said, 'Craig, there's all swear words in our songs! They shouldn't be hearing that fucking stuff!'"

The Fall's latest material was both raunchy and, as everyone commented at the time, more accessible than ever. Crowds rose in expectation to the bass intro of '2 By 4', and the manic rush of 'Lay Of The Land'. These were The Fall's anthems for 1984, just as 'Fiery Jack' and 'Eat Y'Self Fitter' had been clarion calls in their day. And when it appeared in October of that year, the album 'The Wonderful And Frightening World Of . . . ' simply exploded any doubts that one might have harboured about The Fall having either sold out or dried up. Both of these criticisms had been voiced around the reformation time of 'C.R.E.E.P.'.

Brix, September 1985

PAINTWORK THE PAY-OFF

Brix E. Smith was speaking for the rest of the band when she told Tony Clayton-Lea of *Hot Press* that the new LP was in many ways The Fall's revenge. "It's the best thing so far, ever," she affirmed. "I'm really proud, and I know Mark is. I know the whole band is. I think this record can stand up to anything, and any kind of criticism. I have complete faith in it. I think that finally, we've gotten into a good record company and they're taking care of us. Things are looking up, y'know? This shows in our music."

Released simultaneously with the 'Call For Escape Route' EP, plus the gimmicky but welcome 'Slang King' freebie, 'The Wonderful And Frightening World Of (The Fall)' earned the group much deserved praise. *NME* writer Mat Snow was just one of many who commended the band's manifest progress.

"More than ever," he believed, "Fall songs work tangentially, allusively and associatively – buzzwords and trigger-phrases bowled out with varying degrees of spin applied by the curl of Mark Smith's lip. Beneath and above all, there wells a roaring musical current of disgust and loathing, a sociopathic revelling in today's crappy world of back-biting, snarl-ups, deadlock, double-talk, paranoia and recrimination. Such intensity of weltschmerz abstracted into music I find headily compelling, even invigorating in a ruthless way . . . After a Fall record, just about any other piece of music sounds trite and sentimental."

What also came across on 'Wonderful And Frightening',

Karl Burns & Mark Smith, September 1985

as it had done on 'C.R.E.E.P.', was Brix's vocal presence. Though relatively understated, her voice added an extra, and much needed, dimension from husband Mark's point of view. "The balance is finally right inside the group," he asserted, "both in attitude and music. I always felt The Fall were a bit weak vocally compared to the instrumental side of it, and Brix is tightening that up. And she's writing a lot of the new music and that's changing the way I write words."

Brix, whose assertive style of playing owed much to her having formerly been a bass player, put more emphasis on her guitar contributions. She told Tony Clayton-Lea of *Hot Press* why she thought her approach was different. "Most girl guitarists are much too sensitive," she declared. "Without balls. I like to try to give it balls and sound sensitive. I hope that doesn't sound crude, but it's the only way I can explain it."

On-stage, Brix was dwarfed by her Rickenbacker guitar. Yet her presence was such that she was undoubtedly a second focal point for the audience. Pretty, trim, with a swirling head of hair, Brix often pulled attention off-centre, especially when she gave in to the male portion of the crowd's clamouring for her ritually discarded plectrum. In interviews, too, Brix now more than made up for the other musicians' reticence when she added her voice to that of M.E.S. To paraphrase 'Slang King', this was Mr and Mrs Smith to whom you were speaking. Investing her with unprecedented importance, *Sounds*' reporter Jack Barron concluded that Brix was more than just an integral member of the band.

"Brix," he wrote, "has turned The Fall from an enclosed cult into a public phenomenon, and she has fundamentally shifted The Fall's soundscape with pop devices. This is no bad thing and on the 'Wonderful And Frightening' set the sonic symbiosis was complete. Denseness was unfolded, but the lyrical inscrutability and overwhelming musical instinct of The Fall remained intact."

For nearly seven years The Fall's music and their being had percolated down into the various strata of the nation's sub-culture. Though they tried to distance themselves from any so-called underground movement, they couldn't deny that The Fall continued to exert an influence on the super-saturated 'alternative' scene. Such pre-eminence became on occasion a source of embarrassment to Mark E. Smith, who was slowly being regarded as one of rock's elder statesmen.

"I don't really consider myself a musician," he apologised. "I'm deeply ashamed that my passport says 'Songwriter/Musician', there's some vague affectation about it."

PAINTWORK **THE PAY-OFF**

Mark & Brix

Smith was also wary of the trap of acceptance, the point where The Fall and all their careers would be sustained through reputation alone. There was always a danger that the name might transcend the faults and the merits of the material they produced. Too many once-notable bands (authors, actors, painters, comedians) outstayed their welcome for this very reason. This knowledge, coupled with interest in The Fall's work now coming from sources other than those in the music business, saw Mark E. Smith embark on two entirely new projects. David Byrne of Talking Heads had made similar movements away from the rock industry with *The Catherine Wheel* and *The Knee Plays*.

The first of these projects was for Smith and the rest of the band the most intriguing. They had been approached by a young Mohicaned Scot by the name of Michael Clark who wished to perform a ballet featuring 'Kicker Conspiracy' and 'New Puritan'. Unable to imagine the outcome of such an unlikely pairing, Smith gave his consent to the songs being used and the Royal Ballet renegade duly donned his Doc Marten boots. Brix was thrilled. She warmed to the fact that preconceptions of both the pro-Fall faction and those who had come to see Michael Clark, rising star of dance, were being challenged.

"Michael's choreographed half his new ballet to our songs," she told *Sounds*' man Andy Hurt. "People who would never have even considered listening to The Fall have gone out and bought our records. It works in other ways, too, for people who are prejudiced against ballet. It's great to put things together that initially seem incompatible and make them work."

Besides sharing a capacity for drinking large quantities of alcohol, Clark, like Smith, had a preference for playing to conservative audiences rather than "the trendy left-wingers at The Riverside or the ICA."

When he eventually teamed up with The Fall for a live performance, the results were seen on BBC 2's rock showcase *Whistle Test*. The post-mortem was also held on television, when the now legendary 'bare bum routine' was rubbished by Ludovic Kennedy's guests on *Did You See?*, though in all fairness most of the criticism was levelled at the accompanying 'noise'.

"It was a nightmare," Clark told *Melody Maker*'s Tom Morton. "It didn't work at all. We wanted to integrate what we were doing with the band, but we were rushed."

The Scottish Ballet Company's 1985 production *Hail The Classical* was the first successful Fall/ballet fusion. Using the song title 'The Classical' as a starting point Clark was, as Tom Morton put it, "coercing audiences into re-examining the sacred cows of ballet."

One act during this sustained parody featured a gigantic strap-on penis, which Glasgow Theatre's shocked management banned from matinée performances. Clark further assaulted the audience's senses with an array of outlandish, hybrid costumes and cacophonous interplay between Ravel and The Fall over the auditorium speakers. The Fall's music, he claimed, enabled him to explore the extremes.

"I went to see him do one in Manchester," Smith recalled to *Smash Hits*' William Shaw. "That was quite funny because all the audience were in dickie-bows and blue rinses. They had our music on the speakers and they couldn't cope with it. All the people were trying to clap along politely to this DANG-DANG-DANG-CRASH!! Except for this one old woman who had her hands over her ears. Fabulous."

Later collaborative works were staged at the Edinburgh Fringe Festival, perhaps Britain's premier arts venue, a strange arena in which to experience the strident music of The Fall.

The second venture, begun in 1985, was the publication of a book of Fall lyrics. Collated in Germany by Wulf Teichmann, under the guidance of Mark E. Smith, *The Fall Lyrics* promised to be the quintessential Fall document, the ideal companion for one's "lousy record collection." While it contained entertaining press releases and the like, the 20 or so actual lyrics it detailed meant that it was not the exhaustive volume fans hungered for. The period 1977 to 1983 covered by the book had produced easily 10 times this amount of material. Fans could only hope that Smith had plans for a comprehensive and updated edition.

Brix's sole extra-Fall activity was her band The Adult Net, a mysterious bunch of allegedly well-known musicians who débuted in June 1985 with Strawberry Alarm Clock's 1967 psychedelia hit 'Incense And Peppermints'.

Promotional posters also advertised The Fall's latest single 'Couldn't Get Ahead', a slice of bedlam featuring Steve Hanley's stand-in, Simon Rogers, on bass guitar. Hanley had taken a temporary vacation from the band as there was a baby on the way, during which time he worked in a petrol station, where the pay was an improvement on being employed in The Fall. On his return Mark Smith asked him whether he had enjoyed the change.

"No," Hanley had replied. "I really missed being in the group. I missed it like fuck."

On the subject of money, Smith dearly wished that The

Fall could make enough money for him to be able to reward the band for their unfailing loyalty: "They've stuck by me and I appreciate that. Tough lads as well. I like tough, mature people."

The year culminated with The Fall renewing their acquaintance with rock video, the band going the whole hog in their promotion of the new single 'Cruiser's Creek'. During filming, the band had to send out a plea over the Virgin megastore tannoy for extras. The song itself was about the time when Mark E. Smith used to work in an office. "It is a sort of macabre office party," he explained to *Record Mirror*'s Andy Strickland, "where at the end, you don't know if the people are left alive or not or whether somebody left the gas on. It's a party lyric with an evil twist."

Smith confessed to enjoying the role of director, shouting orders at everyone through his megaphone, but he expressed his doubts about the group having anything to do with videos.

"I intended to make it a film as opposed to your normal pop video," learned *Melody Maker* writer Barry McIlheney. "Then we could stop having to do any videos at all! Anyway, I thought if we could do this film with no lip-sync or any shite like that and not have it linked to any particular song then the next time some bastard says, 'You can't get on my show because you don't have a video,' we can send him this one. Send it all over the world and use it for every record we ever release!"

Despite the shoestring budget on which 'Cruiser's Creek' was produced, Smith said that he would much rather have had the money to divide among the group. One consolation was that other bands less popular than The Fall would waste thousands of pounds on a video that the public would only ever see a 10-second clip of on *The Tube*.

Unable to help himself, and despite telling everyone that it was old hat to do so, Mark E. Smith continued to rail against bands, especially the newer ones who had, as it were, overtaken The Fall: "I mean, can you imagine? Sitting there for weeks writing, 'Hello, I'm Micky from The Alarm.' Like, who gives a shit?"

Neither could he stand being patronised by "these brats who want to be the next Smiths or Pale Fountains or whatever – none of their songs have the imagination or scope of what we did years ago when we were fuckin' hungry." And in the next breath he would be warning them of the perils of crippling tax bills. Speaking to *NME*'s Mat Snow, Smith said that he wouldn't be inclined to start a group in the present artistic climate.

"It's too bloody easy," he grouched. "Too bloody

Mark Smith, September 1985

Brix, Mark & Karl, Deutschland, September 1985

encouraged; too bloody like something you do because you're unemployed. You get on a Manpower Services Commission scheme if you want to form a band these days – they give you fuckin' £40 a week! Bloody pathetic. You go play to the council and they give you a cheque for it. Fuckin' joke . . . Yes, it does piss me off that all these people are getting government grants for starting a bloody band – we're culturally important!"

When Smith's outspokenness spilled over into the realm of what he called "cosy charity gigs", interviewers like *Melody Maker*'s Barry McIlheney were shocked to silence. In the aftermath of the Ethiopian famine and *Live Aid*, when The Fall were adamantly refusing to play free festivals, Smith's views did seem to be at odds with the entire Western Hemisphere. "I smell a lot of Victorian bloody do-gooding about the whole thing," he said.

PAINTWORK **THE PAY-OFF**

"There are people in Hulme who are half-starved, so why not send the aid to them? Never in a million years . . . And any country that can be invaded by the Italian army must be a load of crap. Am I right?"

Smith and Company had been touring on the Continent, out of harm's way, when the imperiously-titled album 'This Nation's Saving Grace', appeared in the shops. On their way to more receptive German audiences The Fall had stopped off in Belgium, where Mark E. Smith nearly got his comeuppance.

"I was on stage," he recalled, "and we were barely into the set when suddenly the music stops and there's this guy in a funny uniform standing beside me with a fuckin' revolver against my head. I thought, 'Oh, this guy can't be a cop because the uniform is so stupid, it's just some local lunatic.' So I said, 'Fuck off' and went on singing. Then they cut the power off all of a sudden and he said to me, 'Turn it down or I'll shoot you in the fucking head.' Seriously. They're really screwed up, the Belgians."

Suffice to say, he lived to read the reviews of 'This Nation's Saving Grace' and run the gauntlet of interviews that accompanied every album release. Discussing the LP, Smith revealed how the band had had an earlier close shave, again involving Belgium. It had happened at the time of the Heysel Stadium disaster in Brussels when a riot between Liverpool and Juventus fans left nearly 40 people dead before the European Cup Final. The Fall were scheduled to tour Italy but were forced to cancel at the last minute because the organiser hadn't supplied them with return air tickets. Disappointment turned to relief as they watched the game on television.

"We were due to play in Juventus' home town Turin the day after the match," *NME*'s Richard Cook was told. "Can you believe it? So close! Imagine being in a Turin hotel, in dorms, with no locks on the doors, and they're burning flags in the fuckin' street!"

'Paintwork' contained a reference to the incident, which Smith thought highlighted the song's montaged form. Originally recorded on a four-track in Simon Rogers' spare room, Smith later listened to the tape in a hotel unaware that the cassette player was broken.

"I turned it off and it was still recording," he explained. "Then I saw the red light was still on so I hit it off because it was erasing the song. The funny thing was I was watching the telly and singing along to the song while it was recording. It fits in really good: you can't contrive something like that. It was written like that, too. Things my mother said to me on the night of the Brussels tragedy. I was feeling bad about cancelling the Italian tour and she said, 'Well, you never know with them Continentals, they're little monkeys'."

Brix, 'This Nation's Saving Grace' European Tour, Summer 1985

'Paintwork' was the embodiment of the happy accidents and deliberate design that played such a vital part in the making of every Fall album. It was also the only understated track on 'This Nation's Saving Grace'. The remainder hammered along in the same thunderous vein as 'Cruiser's Creek', all classic Fall riffs backed by Karl Burns' impeccable drumming. *Sounds*' Edwin Pouncey described their 1985 LP as "rump vinyl rock meat, the ideal alternative diet to wimpy vegan pop." And from 'Bombast' through to 'I Am Damo Suzuki', Smith's vocals were indeed in danger of being buried beneath a wall of sound.

"What I was trying to do," he said in defence of the production, "was to bring out the unintelligibility which is missing from all other records these days, where you can hear every syllable of every lyric. I find that quite sickening. It takes away all the mystery, which is half the fun of music in the first place."

Nature had assisted during the recording of 'Barmy', altering Smith's voice through a bad chest infection caused by smoking and not eating properly. At one point it looked as if he would have to go into hospital, but he soldiered on.

"You could hear this rattle of phlegm," he said with pride. "But it sounds good, it sounds better than if I'd done it straight."

The Fall began 1986 with a new drummer, young Simon Wolstencroft, as Karl Burns followed Paul Hanley out of the fold, the latter having departed shortly after 'Wonderful And Frightening'. The year progressed steadily with a spate of singles – 'Living Too Late', 'Mr Pharmacist' and 'Hey! Luciani' – and the usual round of European touring. 'Mr Pharmacist', a cover version of The Other Half's 1960's amphetamine anthem, did reasonably well in reaching number 75 in the charts, but its subject material wasn't likely to get The Fall invited on to *Top Of The Pops*.

"No free prescriptions for guessing what this song's about!" jibed *Sounds*' Jack Barron. Its position was improved later in the year when 'Hey! Luciani' reached the dizzying heights of number 59, sales perhaps spurred on by the success of the enormously popular album 'Bend Sinister'. Released in October of 1986, 'Bend Sinister' proved to be the biggest-selling Fall album to date, reaching a high point of 36.

Included on their latest LP was 'Mr Pharmacist', probably the most unsubtle song with which The Fall could openly declare an involvement with drugs. It brazenly flew in the face of the Government's current campaign against drug abuse, centred on heroin, which at the time was given so much moral support from a legion of reformed user pop stars. Smith agreed that it was a horrible drug.

"Have you ever seen anyone on heroin?" he asked. "They sweat and snuffle like little piglets. Imagine paying money to be like that – you'll find out what it's like when you're 90, anyway."

Mark E. Smith, the man with "the psychic nose", had never made a secret of the fact that speed fuelled many Fall songs. Whether pro, anti or indifferent, 'No Xmas For John Quays', 'Rowche Rumble', 'Your Heart Out', 'Gramme Friday', 'Middle Mass' and 'Pat-Trip Dispenser' were all peppered with references to the substance. Hallucinogens, too, had appeared on 'Two Steps Back', 'Cary Grant's Wedding', and more recently as the 'weird paper' that finished off 'Pat-Trip Dispenser'. The psychedelic spiral on The Fall backdrop at gigs also had hallucinogenic overtones, but Smith assured *NME*'s Gavin Martin that he had ceased his part-time acid demon activities years ago.

"I liked to go places," he said, "do things with it. But now I couldn't handle it. It was a funny time in my life, but it was good to have, a shame to lose it in a way."

In having experimented with drugs, Smith had cultural precedent on his side. Apart from the sad examples of Jimi Hendrix and Sid Vicious, famous writers had long extolled the virtues of attaining an altered state. Novelist Aldous Huxley, author of the discursive essay *Doors Of Perception*, departed from this earth in a serene, mescaline-induced haze.

Smith defended his own position by maintaining that chemical intoxication, like the consumption of alcohol (references to which were probably twice as numerous in Fall songs), was up to the individual. This attitude could have easily been seen as irresponsible, but he was absolutely correct in defending Culture Club's Boy George when the tabloids accused him of inciting impressionable teenage fans to take drugs.

"I don't understand how he can be held responsible for influencing his fans," argued Smith. "I like Elvis Presley records, some of them anyway, but it doesn't mean I'm going to start eating five hamburgers a day."

'Bend Sinister' again came close to the knuckle when the subject of one of Smith's songs was kidnapped in Beirut. Of all the ironies that had befallen the band over the years, the disappearance of the Archbishop of Canterbury's globe-trotting envoy, Terry Waite, just months after the harmless jest of 'Terry Waite Sez' surely had no equal. By comparison, the impact of such an excellent pop tune as 'Shoulder Pads' was destined to be short-lived.

The Brix E. Smith composition 'US 80's – 90's', rooted in the styles of heavy dancefloor music, probed The Fall's not too distant future. With all their Beggars Banquet albums having also been released on compact disc, the band were becoming that much further removed from their

Promoting 'The Frenz Experiment', HMV Shop, Oxford St, London, May 1988

primitive roots. Speaking of the album's more impenetrable material – 'Riddler!', 'Realm Of Dusk', 'Doctor Faustus' – *NME*'s Gavin Martin viewed such development as inevitable and welcome.

"The Fall cover their tracks quickly," he wrote. "As times have got more complex, the literal-mindedness and dogma of their peers has been rejected. The feisty rumble and angular approach of old has grown into a clenched mire of sound, trapping you deeper than ever into Smith's universe; a fine policy for Britain's most consistently imaginative and inventive rock band, now exploring the virtues of implosion as well as explosion, intimacy as well as animation."

This held equally true for the first of 1988's two albums 'The Frenz Experiment'. And the title track 'Frenz' was the most personal song Mark E. Smith had ever committed to vinyl. In 'The Classical' he had sung, 'There are but 12 people in the world, all the rest are paste,' but it didn't match the melancholy with which he now intoned the words, 'My friends ain't enough for one hand, my friends don't amount to one hand . . .'

'Frenz' displayed emotional maturity which really had nothing to do with the Peter Pan world of pop music. Only Talking Heads' David Byrne had similarly embraced the bare necessities of life, most notably on the album 'Little Creatures', where he acceded to the joys of his age and sang quite unashamedly about love between man and woman, and about babies.

In recent years, Smith had begun to touch literally on matters closest to home. In 'No Bulbs' and 'My New House' he had revealed more about himself than in dozens of crabbed rants. Now past 30, Smith was beyond making comments in his music about contentious issues, this he left to the new wave of angry young men like That Petrol Emotion. His vision had become intensely personal and justifiably self-serving. One suspected that both the mellowing and hardening effects of age and marriage, rather than some vague dissatisfaction with the industry, would ultimately be responsible for taking Smith out of the music business. There were many more important things in life than being a rock star. 'Mark'll Sink Us' was a realisation of that end.

When The Fall finally split, Mark E. Smith would not be found rattling through the bins in Tin Pan Alley or roaming along its gutters. Words and a fertile imagination were, after all, his forte. One only had to listen to the involved plot of 'Oswald Defence Lawyer' or the sinister happenings in 'Athlete Cured', on 'The Frenz Experiment', to realise that.

In the meantime, the perennial question of survival continued to be met head-on with punchy singles like 'Hit The North', though the various mixes and formats in

Steve Hanley, Brix Smith, September 1985

which it appeared drew attention to the most annoying aspect of current marketing methods.

Both Beggars Banquet and The Fall seemed happy to go along with the fad for encouraging fans to 'get the set!', picture discs and all. For a band that once fulminated against any kind of gimmickry, The Fall were as guilty as Scritti Politti or any other band for that matter with a fetish for superfluous remixes.

The Fall were just as pragmatic when it came to releasing retrospective albums, and more especially cover versions, stating that everyone else had been supplementing their income in this manner for years. Having broken the ice with 'Rollin' Dany' and 'Mr Pharmacist', The Fall soon followed up with 1987's updated version of R. Dean Taylor's 'There's A Ghost In My House'. Smith wrapped his entire body around the line, 'There's a spectre in my heart' and somehow managed to anglicize the entire song by substituting 'tea' for 'coffee' so that the tortured lover now instead of looking down in his coffee cup, looked down in his tea cup. Subtle but effective.

The band were still unrepentant when 'Victoria', the natural out-take from 'The Frenz Experiment', appeared less than a year later. A fine rendition, but when every other song in the Top 30 seemed to be a cover, it did undermine the achievement. But as Mark Smith told *Smash Hits*' reporter William Shaw, The Fall weren't out there desperately trying for a hit. As ever, they were just taking another step.

"Everybody asks if I'm upset that we've never sold more records," said Smith. "Do people think I'm bloody stupid? Do they think that each time we put a single out I go, 'Oh no! Not again! I haven't got a hit! What am I doing wrong?' My word, I'm not that daft . . . Neither am I going to go moping around like Simply Red did for years saying, 'We're so fucking good and we're not number one in America,' you know what I mean?"

In the day to day cycle of making ends meet, what did rile Smith was other acts undercutting The Fall. He made the poignant observation to *NME*'s Richard Cook that supposedly non-competitive independent groups like Red Wedge were invariably worse than out-and-out commercial bands. "It's always the ones who go on about oppression in

At work on 'Van Plague,' 1988

Thatcher's Britain who are the biggest price cutters."

Whatever the hardships, The Fall had endured. Stamina, both on stage and off, had contributed to their longevity, sustained by engagingly raw music and a rhythmic powerhouse. In Mark E. Smith The Fall had a genuinely original songwriter. What he lacked in vocal talent he more than made up for in the creative department. And The Fall were always at their best when they pushed the outside of that creative envelope, never really playing it safe or ducking and diving into recognised styles.

The Fall's eager participation in 'I Am Curious, Orange', displayed more wit, grit and intelligence than any of their contemporaries. As U2 conquered the world with their slick rock movie *Rattle And Hum*, Michael Clark and The Fall opened in Amsterdam with an unorthodox ballet about the ascendancy of William Of Orange to the British throne. In short, there was no comparison.

The ballet's soundtrack 'I Am Kurious, Oranj' may not have been The Fall's greatest album, but it did speak volumes for their ability and willingness to change. By 1988, The Fall looked, and sometimes sounded, more like a travelling circus than a rock band, with Smith as Master of Ceremonies.

Newcomer Marcia Schofield, who maintained the random keyboard output, had the stature of a fire-eater; Brix was given to wearing a tu-tu; Scanlon and Hanley wrestled with their instruments, and Wolstencroft performed acrobatic feats on the drums. The Fall had allowed the visual influence of Clark to transform them just enough to jar the senses: any more and it would have degenerated into a fancy dress party. This was the realm into which The Fall were moving. Definitions became blurred.

"I do think you have to be aware of the fact that The Fall have always been ahead of their time," Smith told *NME*'s Don Watson, "because it's realising that which will give us the impetus to move forward."

As The Fall progressed, they invented their own rules with which to play the music industry game. Where lesser bands had caved in to rockbiz diktat, The Fall's lack of even the most basic compromise enabled them to retain their independence. But they didn't let their unique position go to their heads. They used it instead to expose the philistinism which had again become endemic within music, within British culture itself. As *NME* writer Barney Hoskyns said: "In the absolute sense, The Fall do not belong in the same universe as your average favourite pop groups. They do not fit in the marketplace of mild equivalences. They show up virtually the whole of the rest of rock as a gross, illusory hype."

Indeed, The Fall are in a world of their own.

SINGLES

It's The New Thing/Various Times
Step Forward SF9 November 1978

Rowche Rumble/In My Area
Step Forward SF11 July 1979

Fiery Jack/2nd Dark Age/Psykick Dancehall No 2
Step Forward SF13 January 1980

How I Wrote Elastic Man/City Hobgoblins
Rough Trade RT048 July 1980

Totally Wired/Putta Block
Rough Trade RT056 September 1980

Lie Dream Of A Casino Soul/Fantastic Life
Kamera ERA001 November 1981

Look, Know/I'm Into CB
Kamera ERA004 April 1982

Marquis Cha Cha/Papal Visit
Kamera ERA014 October 1982

The Man Whose Head Expanded/Ludd Gang
Rough Trade RT133 June 1983

Kicker Conspiracy/Wings/Container Drivers/New Puritan
Rough Trade RT143 October 1983 (Doublepack single)

Oh! Brother/God-Box
Beggars Banquet BEG110 June 1984

Oh! Brother (Extended version)/Oh! Brother/God-Box
Beggars Banquet BEG110T (12") June 1984

C.R.E.E.P./Pat-Trip Dispenser
Beggars Banquet BEG116 August 1984

C.R.E.E.P. (Extended version)/C.R.E.E.P./Pat-Trip Dispenser
Beggars Banquet BEG116T (12") August 1984

No Bulbs No.3/Slang King No.2
Beggars Banquet BEG120 October 1984
(Issued free with Call For Escape Route E.P.)

Couldn't Get Ahead/Rollin' Dany
Beggars Banquet BEG134 July 1985

Couldn't Get Ahead/Rollin' Dany/Petty Thief Lout
Beggars Banquet BEG134T (12") July 1985

Cruiser's Creek/L.A.
Beggars Banquet BEG150 October 1985

Cruiser's Creek/Vixen/L.A.
Beggars Banquet BEG150T (12") October 1985

Living Too Late/Hote After Shave Bop
Beggars Banquet BEG165 July 1986

PAINTWORK **DISCOGRAPHY**

Living Too Late/Hot After Shave Bop/Living Too Long
Beggars Banquet 165T (12") July 1986

Mr Pharmacist/Lucifer Over Lancashire
Beggars Banquet BEG168 September 1986

Mr Pharmacist/Lucifer Over Lancashire/Auto Tech Pilot
Beggars Banquet BEG168T (12") September 1986

Hey! Luciani/Shoulder Pads
Beggars Banquet BEG176 December 1986

Hey! Luciani/Entitled/Shoulder Pads
Beggars Banquet BEG176T December 1986

There's A Ghost In My House/Haf Found Bormann
Beggars Banquet BEG187 May 1987

There's A Ghost In My House/Sleep Debt Snatches/Mark'll Sink Us/Haf Found Bormann
Beggars Banquet BEG187T (12") May 1987

Hit The North Pt 1/Hit The North Pt 2
Beggars Banquet BEG200 October 1987

Hit The North Pt 1/Hit The North Pt 2
Beggars Banquet 200P October 1987 (Picture disc)

Hit The North Pt 1/Australians In Europe/Hit The North Pt 3/Northerners In Europe
Beggars Banquet BEG200T (12") October 1987

Hit The North Pt 4/Hit The North Pt 5/Hit The North Pt 1
Beggars Banquet BEG200TR (12") November 1987

Victoria/Tuff Life Boogie
Beggars Banquet BEG206 January 1988

Victoria/Guest Informant/Tuff Life Boogie/Twister
Beggars Banquet BEG206C January 1988 (Cassette single)

Victoria/Guest Informant/Tuff Life Boogie/Twister
Beggars Banquet BEG206T (12") January 1988

Mark'll Sink Us/Bremen Nacht Run Out
Beggars Banquet FALL 1 March 1988
(Issued free with The Frenz Experiment L.P.)

Jerusalem/Acid Priest 2088/Big New Prinz/Wrong Place Right Time No 2
Beggars Banquet FALL2B (2 x 7" limited edition box set) November 1988

EPS

Bingo Master's Breakout
Psycho Mafia/Bingo-Master/Repetition
Step Forward SF7 July 1978

Call For Escape Route
Draygo's Guilt/Clear Off!/No Bulbs
Beggars Banquet BEG120E October 1984

The Peel Session 27/11/78
Mess Of My . . ./Put Away/No Xmas For John Quays/Industrial Estate
Strange Fruit SFPS028 June 1987

ALBUMS

Live At The Witch Trials
Frightened/Crap Rap 2 – Like To Blow/Rebellious Jukebox/No Xmas For John Quays/Mother-Sister!/Industrial Estate/Underground Medicin'/Two Steps Back/Live At The Witch Trials/Futures And Pasts/Music Scene
Step Forward SFLP1 March 1979

Dragnet
Psykick Dancehall/A Figure Walks/Printhead/Dice Man/Before The Moon Falls/Your Heart Out/Muzorewi's Daughter/Flat Of Angles/Choc-Stock/Spectre Vs Rector/Put Away
Step Forward SFLP4 October 1979

Totale's Turns (It's Now Or Never) (Live)
Fiery Jack/Rowche Rumble/Muzorewi's Daughter/In My Area/Choc-Stock/Spectre VS Rector No 2/Cary Grant's Wedding/That Man/New-Puritan/No Xmas For John Quays
Rough Trade ROUGH10 April 1980

Grotesque (After The Gramme)
Pay Your Rates/English Scheme/New Face In Hell/C'n'C-S Mithering/The Container Drivers/Impression Of J. Temperance/In The Park/W.M.C. – Blob 59/Gramme Friday/The N.W.R.A.
Rough Trade ROUGH18 November 1980

Slates
Middle Mass/An Older Lover Etc/Prole Art Threat/Fit And Working Again/Slates, Slags Etc/Leave The Capitol
Rough Trade RT071 (10" LP) April 1981

Hex Enduction Hour
The Classical/Jawbone And The Air Rifle/Hip Priest/Fortress-Deer Park/Mere Pseud Mag. Ed./Winter (Hostel-Maxi)/Winter No 2/Just Step S'Ways/Who Makes The Nazis/Iceland/And This Day
Kamera KAM005 March 1982

Room To Live
Joker Hysterical Face/Marquis Cha Cha/Hard Life In The Country/Room To Live/Detective Instinct/Solicitor In Studio/Papal Visit
Kamera KAM011 October 1982

Perverted By Language
Eat Y'self Fitter/Neighbourhood Of Infinity/Garden/Hotel Bloedel/Smile/I Feel Voxish/Tempo House/Hexen Definitive-Strife Knot
Rough Trade ROUGH62 December 1983

The Wonderful And Frightening World Of . . .
Lay Of The Land/2 By 4/Copped It/Elves/Slang King/Bug Day/
Stephen Song/Craigness/Disney's Dream Debased (Cassette version
also includes O! Brother/Draygo's Guilt/God Box/Clear Off!/
C.R.E.E.P./Pat-Trip Dispenser/No Bulbs)
Beggars Banquet BEGA58 October 1984

This Nation's Saving Grace
Mansion/Bombast/Barmy/What You Need/Spoilt Victorian Child/
L.A./Gut Of The Quantifier/My New House/Paintwork/I Am Damo
Suzuki/To Nkroachment: Yarbles (Cassette version also includes
Vixen/Couldn't Get Ahead/Petty Thief Lout)
Beggars Banquet BEGA67 October 1985

Bend Sinister
R.O.D./Dktr. Faustus/Shoulder Pads No 1/Mr Pharmacist/Gross
Chapel-British Grenadiers/U.S. 80's – 90's/Terry Waite Sez/
Bournemouth Runner/Riddler!/Shoulder Pads No 2
(Cassette and CD also include Living Too Late/Town And Country/
Hobgoblins/Auto Tech Pilot)
Beggars Banquet BEGA75 October 1986

The Frenz Experiment
Frenz/Carry Bag Man/Get A Hotel/Victoria/Athlete Cured/In These
Times/The Steak Place/Bremen Nacht/Guest Informant (excerpt)/
Oswald Defence Lawyer
(Cassette and CD also include Tuff Life Boogie/Twister/Bremen
Nacht Run Out/Guest Informant)
Beggars Banquet BEGA91 October 1988

I Am Kurious Oranj
New Big Prinz/Overture From 'I Am Curious Orange'/Dog Is Life –
Jerusalem/Kurious Oranj/Wrong Place, Right Time/Win Fall CD
2080/Yes, O Yes/Van Plague?/Bad News Girl/Cab It Up!
(Cassette and CD also include Guide Me Soft/Last Nacht/Big New
Priest)
Beggars Banquet BEGA96 October 1988

COMPILATION, RETROSPECTIVE AND IMPORT ALBUMS

Short Circuit – Live At The Electric Circus
Stepping Out/Last Orders
Virgin VCL5003 (10" LP) June 1978

The Early Years 1977 – 1979
Repetition/Bingo Master's Breakout/Psycho Mafia/Various Times/It's The New Thing/Rowche Rumble/In My Area/Dice Man/Psykick Dancehall/Second Dark Age/Fiery Jack
Step Forward SFLP6 September 1981

A Part Of America Therein, 1981
The N.W.R.A./Hip Priest/Totally Wired/Lie Dream Of A Casino Soul/Cash 'N' Carry/An Older Lover/Deer Park/Winter
Cottage Records (Live US import) 1982

In A Hole
Impression Of J. Temperance/The Man Whose Head Expanded/Room To Live/Hip Priest/Lie Dream Of A Casino Soul/Prole Art Threat/Fantastic Life/English Scheme/Joker Hysterical Face/Hard Life In The Country/Jawbone And The Air Rifle/The Classical/Mere Pseud Mag Ed/Marquis Cha Cha/Backdrop/No Xmas For John Quays/Solicitor In Studio
Flying Nun (Live New Zealand import) 1983

Nord-West Gas
My New House/Bombast/Disney's Dream Debased/Couldn't Get Ahead/No Bulbs/Paintwork/C.R.E.E.P./I Am Damo Suzuki/Rollin' Dany/L.A./Barmy/Lay Of The Land
Funf Und Vierzig Records (German import) 1986

Palace Of Swords Reversed
Prole Art Threat/How I Wrote Elastic Man/Totally Wired/Pay Your Rates/Putta Block/An Older Lover Etc/Fit And Working Again/Marquis Cha Cha/The Man Whose Head Expanded/Neighbourhood Of Infinity – live/Kicker Conspiracy/Wings
Cog Sinister COG1 December 1987

Hip Priest & Kamerads
Lie-Dream Of A Casino Soul/The Classical/Fortress/Look Know/Hip Priest/Room To Live/Mere Pseud Mag Ed/Hard Life In The Country/I'm Into CB/Fantastic Life
Situation Two SITU13 March 1988

Sgt Pepper Knew My Father
A Day In The Life
NME PEPLP100 Youth 1988

VIDEO

Perverted By Language Bis
Wings/Totally Wired/Kicker Conspiracy/Hexen Definitive – Strife Knot/Eat Y'self Fitter/Tempo House/The Man Whose Head Expanded/Smile/Draygo's Guilt – Hip Priest (excerpts)/Container Drivers
Ikon Video 1983